D0893835

The Tao of Bowie

Mark Edwards has two parallel careers – as a journalist and as a trainer/life coach.

As a journalist he began his career writing on magazines, including *The Face*, *Arena*, *GQ*, *Esquire* and *Blitz*. For the past 25 years his work has appeared virtually every week in the *Sunday Times*, and for 12 of those years he was the paper's chief pop music critic.

As a coach and trainer, he works with individuals to help them live with more purpose and meaning, and with some of the country's most successful companies, helping them to support and develop future leaders. All his work is informed by mindfulness and the Buddhist insights that underpin it.

These two parallel careers are fused together in *The Tao of Bowie*.

The Tao of Bowie
10 LESSONS FROM DAVID BOWIE'S LIFE
TO HELP YOU LIVE YOURS
Mark Edwards

ALLEN&UNWIN

First published in Great Britain in 2021 by Allen & Unwin

10 9 8 7 6 5 4 3 2 1

A CIP catalogue record for this book is available from the British Library.

Hardback ISBN: 978 1 91163 086 9
E-book ISBN: 978 1 76087 451 3

Designed and typeset by www.benstudios.co.uk

Printed and bound by CPI Group (UK) Ltd, Croydon CR0 4YY

Allen & Unwin
An imprint of Atlantic Books Ltd
Ormond House
26–27 Boswell Street
London
WC1N 3JZ

www.allenandunwin.com/uk

Contents

INTRODUCTION

WHAT IS THIS BOOK ABOUT?

The Tao of Bowie is partly a book about David Bowie. But it's mainly a book about *you*.

It has a simple concept: that David Bowie's lifetime journey of self-discovery can be used as a template for yours; that the powerful ideas that fascinated Bowie and helped to shape his work, his career and his life can help you towards a life of greater happiness and purpose; and that, by following the exercises in this book, you can pursue your own journey to self-discovery using Bowie as an accessible gateway to some of the world's wisest teachings.

WHY DAVID BOWIE?

Bowie was one of the most remarkable cultural figures of the past century. But behind the confident, charismatic artist we all knew was a human being who started out as a young man feeling lost and isolated, unsure of his place in the world, unable to love or be loved. And yet he grew and developed to a point where he found happiness, let love into his life, and was even able to face his final illness with the equanimity and bravery that allowed him to create a final masterwork about his own death, the *Blackstar* album.

This is the Bowie we will examine in this book. Not the beautiful, charismatic, talented global superstar, but the shy young man battling life's challenges – lonely, adrift and desperate for help, support and advice.

If you sometimes find life difficult, if you struggle to find your place in the world, to understand why you're here or to identify your purpose, then Bowie's story is your story. And you can learn from his example.

How did Bowie turn his life around? How did he grow and mature? How did he transcend the near-fatal challenges of his early adulthood to emerge stronger and happier?

We can answer these questions because Bowie was always very open about the ideas and philosophies that he used as the basis of his personal growth – the pick 'n' mix spiritual code that became his North Star, guiding him through his life.

If you would like to make more sense of *your* life, Bowie has, in fact, done a lot of the 'heavy lifting' for you already by cherry-picking an extraordinary collection of ideas from the world's greatest spiritual leaders, philosophers, scientists, psychologists and artists. So much so that following his path can make your own journey of self-discovery that bit easier.

In *The Tao of Bowie* you will find these ideas condensed into ten powerful life lessons, each of which can help you move further along your own journey of self-discovery.

WHERE DO THE TRANSFORMATIVE LESSONS IN THIS BOOK COME FROM?

Bowie's fans know that he was a cultural magpie: borrowing ideas from mime and kabuki theatre, championing little-known singers and bands, beginning concerts with surrealist films, mixing French chansons and English music hall with heavy rock. He was also a *spiritual* magpie, immersing himself in many different wisdom traditions from many different countries, eras and disciplines in search of the help and guidance he needed to make sense of his life.

Bowie studied Tibetan Buddhism before he became famous. Indeed, he very nearly became a Buddhist monk. And the questions that drove him to explore Buddhism also drove him to investigate other Eastern religions including Taoism and Zen, the philosophy of Nietzsche, the psychological theories of Carl Jung, the secrets of the Gnostic gospels and Kabbalah, the absurdist and existential writings of Albert Camus, the controversial yet influential theories of Julian Jaynes, author of *The Origin of Consciousness in the Breakdown of the Bicameral Mind*. And many more. These are the primary sources for Bowie's philosophy of life. *The Tao of Bowie* examines these ideas, explores how they impacted Bowie's life and then explains how they can help you.

This isn't a gimmick. We know that the journey of self-discovery was vital to Bowie. He was consistently clear throughout his life that his songwriting was principally a means for him to carve out his own spiritual path – to ask (and try to answer) his questions about life.

IS THIS BOOK FOR YOU?

In 2002, three decades after he nearly became a Buddhist monk, Bowie told journalist Anthony DeCurtis:

> I honestly believe that my initial questions haven't changed at all. There are fewer of them these days, but they're really important ones. Questioning my spiritual life has always been germane to what I was writing. Always.
>
> It's because I'm not quite an atheist – and it worries me. There's that little bit that holds on. 'Well, I'm *almost* an atheist. Give me a couple of months. I'm almost there.' … It's either my saving grace or a major problem that I'm going to have to confront.

'Almost an atheist'. That's perhaps where a lot of us find ourselves in the modern world. We reject the idea of God as a big bloke with a white beard living in the clouds, but we can't quite ever get to the point where we absolutely, definitely don't believe in anything at all. Like Bowie, we wrestle with the big questions:

> Why am I here?

Is this all there is?

What am I supposed to do with my life?

At some points in our lives, when things are particularly tough, the big questions might become more urgent. We might phrase them slightly differently, slightly more brutally:

What's the point?

Why is life so hard?

What's *wrong* with me?

Why can't I be happy like [insert name of person you know who seems to have life pretty much worked out]?

Are things ever going to go my way?

We each articulate the big questions in our own way: some of us are looking to make some sense of a life that seems to be spinning out of control; others are angry that we haven't got what we wanted out of life; still others are confused because we *have* got what we wanted out of life but still don't seem to be enjoying it. We feel there must be something more to life. Something we don't quite get. Something we *could* get, if we only knew where to look for it.

If any of this resonates with you, then *The Tao of Bowie* is here to help.

We're a cynical, sceptical lot – us almost atheists – and we're suspicious of anything that sounds like superstition or mumbo-jumbo, and frankly horrified at some of the things that have been perpetrated in the name of organized religion.

So we're going to have to set out without the reassuring certainties or explicit commandments of an omniscient deity. What shall we use instead? My suggestion – odd as it may initially sound – is that we use the ideas that Bowie chose to focus on. They are, I contend, an invaluable guide to a life well lived.

By following The Tao (or 'path') of Bowie, you can create your own fascinating, rewarding, and eye-opening passage through life.

THE BENEFITS OF FOLLOWING THE TAO OF BOWIE

The ideas explored in this book – and brought to life in the exercises – come from some of the greatest thinkers of the past three thousand years. They are proven over time, and they are validated by modern neuroscience. As a trainer and a coach, I have watched people work through these ideas and seen their transformative power first-hand.

Every reader will follow the path in their own way, and will experience different benefits as a result. But, broadly speaking, if you commit to working through the exercises, you might expect greater happiness and greater purpose in your life.

Let me explain exactly what I mean by those terms.

By 'happiness' I mean a combination of the following:

Contentment: a greater ability to be 'happy for no reason' rather than pinning your hopes of happiness on external factors that may be outside your control. An ability to feel OK even when things aren't going your way

Equanimity: an ability to cope better with life's problems and challenges, without being thrown off balance

Resilience: an ability to flow with the natural change and uncertainty of life

Peace of mind: a healthier relationship with your thoughts (especially the anxious, negative ones) and feelings (especially the uncomfortable ones)

By 'purpose' I mean:

Self-awareness: a truer understanding of who you really are – the *real* you

Belonging: a stronger sense of how you fit into the world

Values: a clearer articulation of what truly matters to you, and a plan for living aligned to those ideas

Meaning: knowing why you are here and how you can benefit those around you

Those readers who already know something about Buddhism or Taoism will appreciate the irony here; both those wisdom traditions would advise against having any expectations of this book – or indeed any expectations of anything.

This is, indeed, wise advice, and we will examine this idea of living with 'no expectations' in some detail later in the book. But I know that in our goal-driven, time-starved world, you will want to know what you can expect to get out of *The Tao of Bowie*. So I offer the list of benefits above, suggesting that you take them as hints to the general direction we'll be heading in, rather than a precise checklist to be ticked off.

HOW TO USE THIS BOOK

The Tao of Bowie is divided into ten chapters. Each chapter contains one clear life lesson. Each chapter is sub-divided into three sections.

- Bowie's path
- The life lesson
- Your path

Bowie's path focuses on an incident or key theme from David Bowie's life.

The life lesson explains the wise life lesson that we can learn from this moment.

Your path shows you exactly how to apply this lesson to your own life, through a series of exercises, meditations and techniques.

CHAPTER 1: BEGINNINGS

The life lesson: Start your journey of self-discovery now

One day I walked into the Buddhist Society. I went down the stairs and saw a man in saffron robes. He said, in very broken English, 'You are looking for me?' I realized years later that it was a question, but as an eighteen-year-old, I took it as a statement:

'You are looking for me!'

(David Bowie, 2001)

Who are you?

Where are you?

Where are you going?

(Chime YongDong Rinpoche – the man in the saffron robes)

I teach only the cessation of suffering

(Buddha)

BOWIE'S PATH

Four years before his first hit single, David Bowie began an earnest study of Buddhism that would resonate powerfully throughout his work and life.

The young David Robert Jones, an aspiring but, as yet, completely unsuccessful singer-songwriter arrived on the steps of the Buddhist Society in London in 1965. This was a year before he would change his last name to Bowie, four years before his first hit, 'Space Oddity', and seven years before he truly broke through into the national consciousness with his dazzling creation, Ziggy Stardust.

Crucially, it was two years before The Beatles attended Maharishi Mahesh Yogi's Transcendental Meditation seminar in Wales, suddenly and dramatically bringing previously obscure Eastern religions into the spotlight of mainstream popular culture.

When the young David Jones arrived at the Buddhist Society, he was not a wannabe. He was not following some fad that would shine brightly for a few months and then quickly fade. He was carving out his own unique path, one that he would adhere to (in his own way) for the rest of his life.

He had already been interested in Buddhism for some years. His older half-brother, Terry, a huge influence on Bowie in many ways, had introduced him to the work of Jack Kerouac, and the Beats – a literary group who were early Western advocates of Buddhism. Already a voracious reader, David had followed up this initial interest by reading books like Heinrich Harrer's *Seven Years in Tibet* and Lobsang Rampa's *The Rampa Story*.

The first was informative. Harrer, an Austrian who had escaped from a British POW camp in India, had made his way into Tibet, and the book recounted his life as a tutor to the young Dalai Lama. It offered genuine insight into both Tibet and Buddhism.

The Rampa Story was a bit different. While Lobsang Rampa claimed to be a Tibetan holy man, he was, in fact, an unemployed surgical fitter from Devon called Cyril Hoskin. Of course, there's no reason why a surgical fitter from Devon cannot impart great wisdom, but Hoskin's book was a work of fiction.

However, when Bowie entered The Buddhist Society headquarters in 1965, he encountered the real deal. The man with the saffron robes and broken English was Chime YongDong Rinpoche. Born in the remote eastern Tibet region of Kham, and identified at the age of two as a reincarnated lama, he was educated at Benchen monastery from this early age. He was one of a select group of monks who went to China with the Dalai Lama for a fateful visit during which Mao Tse-tung informed them that 'religion is poison'. Shortly afterwards China began a brutal persecution that saw Buddhist monks and nuns murdered and monasteries (including Benchen) destroyed. In 1959, Chime made his escape via Bhutan to India, eventually making his way to the UK – one of just three Buddhist lamas to do so.

Over the next two years, Chime would become Bowie's main teacher, during which time Bowie would come to the Buddhist Society to study up to four times a week. The other two escapees who made it to the UK, Chögyam Trungpa Rinpoche and Akong Rinpoche, moved to Eskdalemuir in Scotland to set up Samye Ling, the first Tibetan Buddhist monastery in Europe, where Bowie would also study.

Indeed, in 1967 Bowie travelled up to Samye Ling with a clear intention. As he later said, 'I was within a month of having my head shaved, taking my vows, and becoming a monk.'

Was this a slight exaggeration by Bowie? We can't be absolutely sure. Certainly there were some points in his career when he was happy to give a provocative quote to journalists in search of a headline; however, when he talked about his spiritual life in interviews he was usually serious and measured. Exactly how determined Bowie was to become a monk we'll never know. But contemporary friends like Mary Finnigan (Bowie's landlady for a time) and associates like journalist George Tremlett (who wrote the first biography of Bowie) note that he was extremely earnest in his studies. Indeed, when Bowie was first introduced to rising young producer Tony Visconti – a man who could potentially help his career (and went on to do so) – the pair didn't talk about studios or demos; they bonded over Buddhism.

Visconti, who has himself retained a lifelong interest in Buddhism, confirms that Bowie's study of the subject was genuine and deep: 'David was definitely a scholar of Tibetan Buddhism. He knew it all. He was a very curious person, a fast reader and rarely forgot information once it was stored in his head.'

WHAT BOWIE LEARNED FROM BUDDHISM

Eventually, it was Chime who talked Bowie out of becoming a monk. But this should not be taken as an indication that Bowie's teacher thought the young man was not serious in his studies. Rather it reflected changing times. Chime often discouraged devoted students of Buddhism from becoming monks or nuns – and both he and Chögyam Trungpa later disrobed – reflecting a belief that, in the West, in the modern world, the idea of isolating yourself in a monastery was outdated and inappropriate.

And even though Bowie chose music over the monastery, there can be no doubting the impact that his studies had on the rest of his life. As he said in 1997, they left him with:

> a sense of transience and change which actually became fundamental to my life and my approach to it. Not holding on to anything – not considering that there is anything that will last through one's entire eternal life – living or dead. And it makes letting go very easy – material things or physical things.
>
> And looking for the source of one's own being becomes much more important. And I guess that's been my own personal journey – trying to sort out where my spiritual bounty lies, where my thread to a universal order lies. That can become a life's search.

The two most important ideas that Bowie took from his Buddhist studies are:

Change: that everything is transient

Looking for the source of one's own being: that investigating your self – the journey of self-discovery – is supremely important

Of these two, the importance of change to Bowie is the most immediately obvious. He wrote one of his most famous songs about it, 'Changes'. And his career was a dazzling succession of changes of style and character. But in *The Tao of Bowie* we will focus on the latter idea, looking at how Bowie undertook his journey of self-discovery and how you can pursue your own journey.

This is by no means an exclusively Buddhist idea. Quite the opposite. The importance of self-investigation is an idea that unites many of the world's great wisdom traditions, even some of those that often find themselves in conflict with each other. Bowie went on to study many of these other wisdom traditions to refine his own personal spiritual code, which guided him through his struggles to eventual happiness.

Bowie retold the story of his meeting with Chime on several occasions. On one of these, he emphasized that he simply *couldn't have allowed himself* to hear Chime's gentle enquiry 'You are looking for me?' as a question. 'I *needed* it to be a statement,' he said. But why was Bowie looking for a guru? Why did he *need* a guru? Because at the tender age of eighteen, he'd already begun what he would later describe as his 'daunting spiritual search'. He was already looking for the source of his own being. He knew from his reading that the Buddhist journey of self-discovery could lead him to a place where his

life would make more sense, where he would understand more about who he really was and how he fitted into the world.
In Chime, he saw a man who might provide him with some answers.

Yet, instead of providing Bowie with answers, in fact, Chime offered him three questions:

Who are you?

Where are you?

Where are you going?

THE LIFE LESSON: START YOUR JOURNEY OF SELF-DISCOVERY NOW

Like Neo in the film *The Matrix*, our 'reality' is not as real as we think. Crucially, our normal sense of 'self' – of who we are – is flawed. The journey to discover our true self is at the heart of our ability to live life to the full.

Bowie had encountered an extraordinary human being. As a reincarnate lama, Chime is a venerated Buddhist master who has received transmissions (teachings) that have been handed down personally from teacher to student over many centuries. But, while he may be intricately linked to an ancient tradition, Chime was also pragmatic about his situation in the mid-1960s. Having arrived in a foreign land where his venerated status back in Tibet was utterly irrelevant to 99.9 per cent of the population, he ended up working in a cafe to make ends meet.

He once recalled a conversation with a co-worker in the cafe (who either misheard, misunderstood or deliberately mispronounced his name):

> 'So, Jimmy, what is this Buddhism?'
>
> 'Buddhism is the end of suffering.'
>
> 'Oh, Jimmy, I need that Buddhism.'

Well, yes. We could all use a little less suffering.

Buddhism – certainly in its Westernized form – is not a religion in the sense that we commonly understand the word. There is no God to worship, and there are no commandments to follow. It's much closer to a form of psychology, a method of working with the mind.

In essence, Buddha noted that people tend to suffer, to be unhappy, dissatisfied and disappointed. And he suggested a method for relieving these symptoms. He said it worked for him, and suggested others tried it too.

There are many forms of Buddhism but, because we know his teachers, we can be clear on which version of Buddhism Bowie studied. He was educated in the Kagyu tradition and the absolute heart of this method is meditation. Indeed, the Kagyu lineage is often referred to as 'the practising lineage' ('practice' being a common term for meditation).

How does meditation help to reduce suffering? By offering a means to self-investigation and self-discovery: a way to form a more accurate understanding of your self and the world around you.

We know from other students that Chime liked to offer people new to the discipline those three questions:

Who are you?

Where are you?

Where are you going?

They may not, at first glance, seem that powerful. But whether you're interested in Buddhism or not, these are three of the most important questions we can ask ourselves.

As a coach, I encourage my clients to step back from their day-to-day problems, issues and challenges to address these three fundamental questions. The more clearly you can answer them, the more skilfully you will be able to navigate all aspects of your life.

And yet most people hardly spend any time thinking about them at all. As Jim Rohn, the motivational author and speaker known as 'the godfather of personal development', once wrote: 'most people spend more time planning their vacations than they do planning their lives'.

Is that true for you? It quite possibly is.

Now that you think about it, does it seem ever so slightly odd? I think it does. Especially as, down the centuries, a succession of very wise people have advised us of the benefits of self-examination and self-discovery.

As well as in his Buddhist studies, Bowie will have encountered the same idea in his reading of the philosopher Nietzsche and the psychiatrist Carl Jung, and his voracious examination of the Gnostic gospels. And beyond the wisdom traditions that we know Bowie explored, the injunction to 'know thyself' is a central idea in many others too, from Socratic philosophy to Confucianism, from Hinduism to the I-Ching, from Christianity ('The kingdom of Heaven is within you' – Jesus) to Islam ('Those who know themselves know their Lord' – Mohammad).

Whether these traditions are based on the idea of a God – or of many Gods or of no God at all – they all agree that the best thing we can do is to examine ourselves. The fact that philosophies and religions that disagree so violently over so many issues all find a place of agreement here must surely mean there is something very special indeed about self-examination.

So why do most of us avoid looking deeply into who we are and tackling the big questions about our lives? Perhaps because we're all too busy these days to take the time to contemplate such weighty matters, too busy with the short term to think about the bigger picture; or perhaps because we don't know how to answer them – so we avoid even thinking about them.

But if you've read this far in the book, then you have at least a nagging suspicion that you deserve to carve out the time it takes to tackle these questions. This book will help you do so.

We will answer them on a straightforward level, working through some simple exercises to get a clearer picture of who you are, how you became the person you are today, what really matters to you, and how you can live a life aligned with your values and filled with meaning and purpose.

And we'll also answer them on a deeper level, using meditation as our primary method of enquiry to dig further into who you really are, to clear our way through the delusions that inflict human beings, and to understand the true nature of self, so that you can live with less suffering and increased happiness.

WHAT'S REALLY REAL?

Buddhism starts with a core idea that our current view of the world is flawed. If we wanted to draw an analogy from popular culture, we would look to *The Matrix*. In this film Morpheus (Laurence Fishburne) reveals to Neo (Keanu Reeves) that the reality in which he has lived his entire life isn't reality at all, but a completely constructed delusion.

Our situation on encountering the Buddhist view of the world is much like Neo encountering the Matrix – with one crucial difference. Neo only had to discover that his view of the world *outside* him was completely wrong; Buddhism tells us that our view of the world *inside* us is flawed too.

'Who are you?' is a much deeper question than it might at first appear. When a Buddhist master asks 'who are you?' they're inviting a more profound answer than 'an accountant from Leeds' or 'a self-starter who loves animals'. They want you to address the fundamental questions of what exactly it is that has been born into your body; how you form your sense of 'self'; where exactly this 'self' resides; and how this 'self' (whatever it is) relates to everyone and everything else.

Buddhism questions our conventional sense of the self in three crucial ways. It suggests that:

1. there is no *fixed* or *permanent* self: like everything else in the universe, you are in constant flux.
2. there is no *boss* in there: no one who is fully in control of things, as we would like to believe we are.

3. there is no *separate* self: you are inextricably linked with the rest of the universe.

The first of these ideas is the easiest to assimilate – we know, for example, that we're 'a different person' when we're hungry, tired, stressed or drunk.

The second is disquieting. And the third one just seems plain wrong: of course we're separate; we can see that. But, as we will examine in Chapter 8, allowing that all these three claims *may* be true will further reduce your anxiety and suffering and further increase your happiness. So it's worth at least attempting the thought experiment that they *might* be correct.

This will be our attitude throughout *The Tao of Bowie*. We're not pursuing any grand truth. We're simply trying out ideas and methods to find some that work for you. This is true to the spirit of the Buddha. Once, in a debate with other religious leaders about exactly what doctrine was right or wrong (documented in *The Sutra of Forty-Two Chapters*), Buddha explained that he really wasn't interested in such arguments: 'I look upon the judgement of right and wrong as the serpentine dance of dragons.'

He was interested only in what *worked* – in what relieved suffering. He had identified the causes of human suffering and a method to alleviate it. He wanted to communicate it on a simple basis: it works for me, try it and see if it works for you. Over the centuries a complex religion has been built up around this simple idea, but in recent years, Western Buddhists – including those within the Kagyu lineage – have dismantled some of this complexity. Western Buddhists are encouraged, as Bowie was, to dip in, try it and take what they think works for them. No need to believe in God or demons; no need to light candles, recite prayers and perform prostrations.

Just take the method that has been shown over the centuries to make people happier, and see if it works for you.

So let's start that process now. Because, while *The Tao of Bowie* is in part a book about Bowie and in part a book about the collection of ideas that he used to shape his life, it is primarily a book about how these ideas can help you on *your* path through life.

YOUR PATH

As you work your way through the exercises in this book, meditation will be a core element of your toolbox, so let's start by getting acquainted with how (and why) we meditate.

The form of Buddhism that Bowie studied – the Kagyu lineage of Tibetan Buddhism – is also, as we have noted, known as 'the practising lineage', underlining the vital role that practising (another term for meditating) plays in it. So this is a natural place for us to start.

Exercise: Breathing meditation

We're going to do this for about five minutes. You can set a timer if you want, or just choose to stop after what seems like five minutes to you. The exact time doesn't matter.

Sit comfortably. The state you're aiming for is often termed 'relaxed alertness'. What does that mean? Well, you want to be comfortable, but not so comfortable that you fall asleep. And you want to be alert, but not so alert that you're stressed or rigid.

Try this: sit up straight and imagine you are a puppet with a string coming out of the top of your head, and that someone is gently pulling the string up so that your head is held aloft but your shoulders don't go up with it. Keep your shoulders relaxed. If that visualization helps, use it. If it doesn't, forget it immediately and just sit comfortably.

Close your eyes. Focus on your breath. What does *that* mean? Well, simply become aware of the fact that you're breathing. Notice each breath as it comes in. And as it goes out. Tune in to the rhythm of your breath. The in breath and the out breath. And the next in breath, and the next out breath. And so on, and so on.

That's the whole thing. Do that for approximately five minutes, then open your eyes.

If that was the first time you've meditated, or even if it wasn't, some thoughts or questions might have occurred to you.

Question: How do I know if I'm focusing on my breath properly?

Some people notice the breath at the nostrils. Some people feel it more clearly at the back of the throat. Some people focus on the breath by following the rising and falling of their belly. If you find the whole idea of focusing on your breath a bit odd, it can help to place a hand on your belly and then simply focus on the rhythmic movement of your hand.

Question: Why am I focusing on my breath anyway?

There are two ways of looking at this one:

1. No reason at all. What we're trying to do is focus on the present moment. But that's a bit abstract. We use the

breath as an anchor, an easier thing to focus on. But really the breath doesn't actually matter.

2. We're focusing on the breath because the breath is vitally important to our lives and yet we routinely ignore it. This is a precious moment of checking in on a crucial bodily function. Not checking in a medical way, just in a way that involves curiosity and gratitude for the astonishing processes that keep us alive.

Choose whichever answer you like.

Question: Why is staying in the present moment so important?

Again, two reasons:

1. Because the past and the future are the home of what Chime called 'unnecessary thoughts'. We spend a lot of our time not in the present moment. Instead, we spend it worrying about the future and thinking about the past. Psychologists have a term for this: 'Rehearse Review Regret'. Note that this is not 'Rehearse, Review, Have A Huge Party To Celebrate All Your Past Successes'. No, it's 'Rehearse Review Regret'. When we look back at the past, we tend to focus on the things that went wrong. And when we look into the future, we tend to focus on the things that might go wrong.

   It's a useful human capacity to be able to look so far into the past and the future. It means that we have the potential to learn from our past actions and plan for the future. Occasionally we do this. But often, we just feel bad about stuff that happened in the past (without learning anything from it) and worry about the future (without making any positive preparation to avert the disasters we're imagining). It's pretty clear that all this is the very definition of 'unnecessary thoughts'. If we can carve out some time in the present moment, we can temporarily rid ourselves of these unnecessary and unhelpful thoughts.

2. Because the present moment is the home of self-discovery. One of our core methods of self-discovery in the exercises throughout this book is simply to stay with things as they are: to counter the normal human instinct to run away from reality into endless distractions. In order to stay with things as they are, we need to be able to stay in the present because… well, because that's where things as they are *are*.

Question: What if I fall asleep?

No problem. If when you shut your eyes and focus on your breath for a few minutes, you immediately fall asleep – or want to – then you are clearly not getting enough sleep. You've just checked in with how you feel in the present moment, and discovered that how you feel in the present moment is exhausted. So, if you can, go and have a nap.

However, if you *always* fall asleep when you meditate, clearly you're not going to get any meditating done, so try meditating at a time when you're not so sleepy. If you can't find a time when you don't want to fall asleep when you're meditating, then this is most likely a sleep problem not a meditation problem. Take a long, hard look at your sleep regime.

Exercise: Noticing thoughts

Now we're going to meditate again. But this time we're going to notice our thoughts.

Unless you've been meditating for a very long time indeed, you will have noticed your thoughts in the first meditation. Although the instruction to focus on your breath sounds simple enough, human beings find it virtually impossible to do this. We close our eyes, we focus on the first breath, we focus on the second breath. And then the next thing we know, we find ourselves thinking about what we're going to have for dinner tonight, or worrying about a work colleague who we believe stitched us up, or trying to remember the name of a minor character in a sitcom we watched ten years ago. By the time we realize that we're not focusing on our breath, we might be on the tenth separate thought in a long cascading chain of thoughts that's gone on for several minutes.

This is what we do.

More correctly, this is what our minds do.

This is why one Buddhist master referred to the modern world as being 'lost in thought'. These are 'unnecessary' thoughts and we seem to spend most of our lives in them. In our process of self-discovery, it's important that we get a better understanding of how our mind works. So we meditate noticing thoughts, getting to understand how this strange situation occurs where

– whatever we might be aiming to do – we can be almost immediately overtaken by unnecessary and unhelpful thoughts that we haven't consciously called into being.

The instructions for this exercise are as before. Sit comfortably in relaxed alertness. Close your eyes. Focus on the breath. The in breath and the out breath. Then the next in breath, then the next out breath. And so on, and so on. Stay with the rhythm of the breath.

And this time, each time you notice that your mind has wandered away from your breath, and that you've started thinking about something, simply say to yourself 'thinking' (in your head, not out loud), and then return your focus to your breath. Next time you find yourself thinking again, do the same: say 'thinking' and return to the breath. Do this for about five minutes, then open your eyes and review what happened.

Question: How do I know if I'm thinking?

When I first started teaching meditation, I was surprised to find that sometimes people who were meditating for the first time reported that they were able to stay totally focused on the breath and were not distracted by thoughts at all. Everything that I had been taught suggested this couldn't possibly be happening. It took me a while to realize that these people were not super meditators or strangely advanced beings, but they were in fact so completely and utterly lost in thought that they *didn't even notice they were thinking any more*.

Let's be clear on what thinking is. It's the incessant commentary that runs inside our head (not 'voices in the head' – just the conversation we all have with ourselves).

If when you start to meditate, you feel bored, that's not a thought. That's simply what's happening in the present moment. But as soon as you start *talking to yourself* (in your head) about the fact that you're bored – 'God, this meditation lark is boring. And I'm probably not even doing it right. How long has it been? Can I stop yet? I've got better things to do with my time' – that's *all* thought. If when you start to meditate you notice a car alarm going off in the distance, that's not a thought. Again, that's direct experience of what's happening in the present moment. If you feel irritated by the car alarm, that's not a thought either. That irritation is what you are experiencing in the present moment. But as soon as you start moaning to yourself about how you can't possibly be expected to meditate with such a racket going on, or plotting revenge against the owner of the car, deciding that all car owners are scum or wishing that you lived somewhere quieter – that's *all* thought.

Some of us are so used to this constant internal conversation that we confuse it with real life. It isn't real life. It is our *commentary* on real life. When we start to understand this, start to understand the difference between direct experience of the world and this constant chatter that *distances* us from life, then we can live our lives more vividly.

Think of an incident in your life so extraordinary that when you described it to others afterwards you used the phrase 'I've never felt more alive'. The chances are this was a moment – the birth of a child, perhaps, or a bungee jump – when the experience and the feelings it generated were so powerful that for a brief, glorious moment the direct experience of what was actually happening in the world replaced the internal chatter of thoughts.

What if you could feel that alive all the time? OK, maybe that sounds like it would be a bit overpowering. But what if you could taste that 'never felt more alive' state more often? If you meditate regularly, you can; you will learn to have a healthier relationship with your thoughts, one in which you are no longer 'lost' in thought but can choose to quieten the chatter of your mind to experience life more directly.

Exercise: Noticing judgement

In this exercise we essentially repeat the *Noticing thoughts* meditation but this time with an additional element. When you notice a thought, see if it contains an element of judgement. If you notice a thought without judgement, just say to yourself 'thinking' and return your focus to the breath. But if you notice a thought that contains an element of judgement, say to yourself 'thinking, judging' and return your focus to the breath.

Thoughts like: 'God, this meditation lark is boring,' or: 'And I'm probably not even doing it right,' or: 'I've got better things to do with my time,' all contain judgement. Whereas thoughts like: 'How long has it been?' and: 'Can I stop?' don't.

Do this for five minutes, then review what happened.

By this point, you should be somewhere between slightly surprised and really quite shocked at how hard it is to stop thinking. And at how judgemental we all are (it's not just you!)

Noticing how judgemental we can all be, and trying to gradually reduce this, can be very helpful. We can start by not judging ourselves for being 'too' judgemental. Again, this isn't about right and wrong – a way we *should* be – it's about moving towards a way of operating in which we can be kinder to ourselves and others.

So let's do some more work in this area.

Exercise: Noticing judgements in your day-to-day life

Take an hour in your everyday life and commit to noticing every time you judge someone or something. Ideally, choose a time when you're going to be out and about. This exercise also works perfectly well if you're just watching TV, snacking and sipping a hot drink.

Judgemental thoughts are thoughts like:

- This is a great cup of coffee.
- Why am I always late?
- What kind of person would wear a jacket like that?
- This train service is crap.
- The weather is even worse than yesterday.
- There must be something better on TV than this.
- I think the third series of *Friends* was the best series.

- Look where you're going, you idiot.
- I can't believe the state of this report.

Any thought with an element of comparison is judgemental. Any thought that implies there is some kind of ideal or standard is judgemental. Judgemental thoughts can be positive as well as negative.

Review: What actually happened?

We have our first tool: the ability to stay in the present moment, non-judgementally, but we also know that we're not great at it yet. That's OK. Nobody is. Once we have an honest assessment of where we are, we can build on that.

When I'm coaching clients, and they're learning new skills or new ways of behaviour, it's important that they have some way of measuring their progress. The following feedback loop – the simplest and clearest that I know – is one adapted from the US Army's After-action Review.

> What did we expect to happen?
>
> What actually happened?
>
> Why was it different?

Although it may seem strange to bring in a tool from the army when we're working with Buddhist meditation, these questions can be very helpful as we track our progress through this book. Take the meditation that we've just been doing.

What did we expect to happen? We expected to focus on our breath.

What actually happened? We couldn't focus on our breath because we kept thinking all the time.

Why was it different? That's a question for you to ponder. As we go through the book, we will try and answer the question. But it's important that you spend some time thinking about it yourself first.

Your path: Going forward

After you've been through the exercises above, try the following.

1. Commit to meditating – noticing thoughts and judgements – for three minutes every day. If you can do it for longer, great; but I don't want anyone to have the excuse that they can't find the time in their day to meditate. You do have three minutes. That's all you need to notice your mind wandering into thought and judgement and to gently bring it back to focus on your breath. Every single time you do that, you are developing a valuable skill.
2. Contemplate why human beings find it so hard to focus on one thing (their breath) for any length of time without thoughts distracting us. What does this tell you about the nature of thinking?

3. Try and spend a period of every day living in a state of non-judgement – or, at least, noticing how much you judge.
4. Ask yourself this question: 'Who am I if I don't judge?' You could rephrase that in other ways if you want. You could ask it as 'Who am I if I have no preferences?' or 'Who am I if I have no likes and dislikes?' But, in one form or another, live with that question for a week.

CHAPTER 2: NEEDS

The life lesson: Honour your unmet needs

Everybody says, 'Oh yes, my family is quite mad.' Mine really is. No fucking about, boy. Most of them are nutty – in, just out of or going into an institution. Or dead.

(David Bowie, 1976)

It was a very cold household... It was as if he was there but not there. There was no sign of affection at any time. I don't think it was a family. It was a lot of people who happened to be living under the same roof.

(Bowie's childhood friend Dudley Chapman)

The little world of childhood with its familiar surroundings is a model of the greater world. The more intensively the family has stamped its character upon the child, the more it will tend to feel and see its earlier miniature world again in the bigger world of adult life.

(Carl Jung, The Theory of Psychoanalysis*)*

BOWIE'S PATH

When Bowie turned up on the steps of the Buddhist Society, what was he looking for? A refuge from the severe mental illness that haunted his family and that he feared would one day engulf him.

Next time you fire up YouTube, take a few moments to check out a truly remarkable human interaction. In a 1979 daytime TV show, David Bowie is interviewed by Mavis Nicholson. Bowie is by now long past his outrageous Ziggy persona. He's neat and tidy. No sticky-up red hair. No make-up. Just a 'sensible haircut' and a suit and tie. But it's important to understand that at this time the mainstream media still treated him as some kind of freak. When he was interviewed by people of older generations, they could often barely conceal their confusion about – and sometimes contempt for – this creature who had shocked the establishment by looking like a space alien and by deliberately and very publicly blurring the lines of sexuality when this simply wasn't done.

Mavis Nicholson is from an older generation. She's clearly not a *fan* of Bowie but she's a wonderful interviewer. She's searching, curious, empathetic and understanding. As a result, Bowie – who begins the interview charming, flirty but elusive – gradually lowers his defences and opens up. And she leads Bowie through what I'm convinced is the most illuminating interview he ever gave.

> Mavis: What painter has influenced you?
>
> David: Erich Heckel.
>
> *[Stalemate. Nicholson has likely never heard of the painter whose work influenced the iconic cover of Bowie's* Heroes *album.]*
>
> Mavis: What writer has influenced you?
>
> David: William Burroughs.
>
> *[Again stalemate. Nicholson tries another tack.]*
>
> Mavis: As a child who influenced you?
>
> David: Donald Duck.
>
> Mavis: Was he your favourite?
>
> David: No, I loathed him. He made me learn how to hate.

Wow! You ask someone for their key childhood influence and they respond with the character who *taught them how to hate!* What does that tell you about their childhood?

Nicholson continues probing, seemingly hoping to coax a more positive, more 'normal' childhood influence out of Bowie. But Bowie doesn't have any. Nicholson goes through a list of beloved childhood characters. Bowie expresses dislike for all of them. The interview continues:

Mavis: Did you have a teddy bear?

David: No. I didn't. I don't think...

At this point, he pauses, breaks eye contact and gazes into the distance. This is a powerful moment. A body language expert would note by his eye movement that he is searching both his thought memory and his emotional memory. He is not only remembering the facts about his early childhood, he is recalling how he *felt*.

I have studied many hours of Bowie interviews, and I've never seen him do this at any other time. He continues: 'I can't remember having anything like that at all. No, I never liked children's things very much.'

The interview continues and goes deeper still (and we will pick it up again when we examine Love in Chapter 9) but for now, this is plenty to be going on with. He has no memory of having a teddy bear or other soft toy – the childhood staple of our culture and understood by psychiatrists to be an important transitional object that helps children to grow and develop healthily. He most valued the character who taught him how to hate. And he never liked children's things very much. Why not? Because Bowie's childhood was not a happy place.

BOWIE'S FAMILY BACKGROUND: 'PSYCHOTIC VULTURES'

This is an understatement. In the liner notes to his *Buddha of Suburbia* album, Bowie wrote: 'my writing has often relied too arbitrarily on violence and chaos as a soft option to acknowledge spiritual and emotional starvation'. On another occasion, in an interview in the mid-1990s, he referred to his family in this way: 'I'm not sure if madness is the word. There's an awful lot of emotional and spiritual mutilation goes on in my family.'

Starvation. Mutilation. A psychiatrist would have a field day. Except Bowie never let a psychiatrist near him because he had seen how little help they had been for the rest of his family: a tortured group of people, beset by mental illness for generations. Indeed, his grandmother, Margaret Burns – watching her daughters' suffering – had proclaimed that the family was 'cursed', declaring that the curse would not be over till they were all dead.

Margaret is remembered by Bowie's cousin Kristina as 'a very cruel woman who took her anger out on everyone around her.' Kristina should know, as she spent much of her childhood being looked after by Margaret because her mother (Margaret's daughter, Una) was regularly in and out of mental hospitals after being diagnosed as schizophrenic in the late 1940s.

Una was not the only one of Bowie's aunts to suffer in this way. Two more of his mother's sisters had similar experiences. Nora was diagnosed as suffering from manic depression and eventually had a lobotomy. The treatment was not only brutal, it was unsuccessful. She remained depressed.

Another sister, Vivian, also suffered a schizophrenic breakdown.

Bowie's mother, Peggy, was never diagnosed with mental illness but she clearly shared at least some of her sisters' demons, and evidently struggled with life. She was cold, unable to express emotions or show any affection. Bowie's first wife, Angela, remembers the grown-up Bowie and his mother as 'pecking at each other like psychotic vultures in [a] closed little house'. She said Peggy was 'as mean as she was miserable', hinting at both the coldness that she displayed towards her son and also the deep sadness that lay behind Peggy's emotional frigidity.

During his childhood Bowie's emotional distress exhibited itself in regular calls to the emergency services, summoning ambulances and – on one occasion – two fire engines to the house because he was 'dying'. It's hard to imagine a more vivid example of a 'cry for help'.

The psychologist Oliver James has written that nowadays 'it is highly probable that both Peggy and her mother would have qualified for a diagnosis of personality disorder', and he explored in some detail the effect this family background would have had on the young David Jones in his book *Upping Your Ziggy*.

But if we want to know the effect that it had on Bowie, we can simply return to the stark and bitterly unhappy words he chose to describe the atmosphere in his family home:

> 'Emotional starvation'.
>
> 'Emotional mutilation'.

BOWIE UNDERSTOOD THAT HIS CHILDHOOD HAD LEFT HIM WITH AN UNMET NEED FOR AFFECTION

It's hardly surprising then that Bowie chose on more than one occasion to recite sections of Philip Larkin's poem 'This Be The

Verse' when he was appearing on TV chat shows. The poem is not the usual fare of chat shows – partly because it's a brutal examination of the fact that each generation passes their own misery on to their children, and partly because it famously contains some very strong language – but it clearly resonated very deeply with Bowie.

On one occasion in an interview with Michael Parkinson in 2002, he first quoted the opening of the poem, the bit that says that we're all fucked up by our parents. He then explained:

> I spent an awful lot of my life… looking for myself, and understanding what I existed for, what it was that made me happy in life, and who exactly I was – and what were the parts of myself I was trying to hide from. A lot of us in show business are pretty dysfunctional, and in huge senses of denial of who we are and where we exist in the world. Some kind of trauma often goes on in our childhood that makes us crave some kind of strange affection.

He then talked about the fact that some people find it extremely difficult to show affection, and that if you have not had affection shown to you, then you too will struggle to show it to others. He concluded: 'My parents were like that. And Larkin's right about that. They pass on a lot of faults.'

A NOTE ON BLAME – AND WHY WE SHOULDN'T DO IT

We've been discussing the unhappiness in Bowie's family – from slight sadness through to severe mental illness. When anyone who does this focuses on the 'nurture' causes of unhappiness (the part played by relatives and other caregivers) rather than the 'nature' causes (the part that our genes may play), they lay themselves open to accusations of parent-bashing. So let's be very clear: this isn't about blame.

Peggy was not to blame for the sadness and emptiness in Bowie's childhood. And Margaret was not to blame for the sadness and emptiness in hers.

Each simply learned the parenting style of their parents and, with a consequently extremely limited emotional capability, passed this on. This is a pattern that may have gone on for many generations. Each generation simply passing on a repeated pattern of not-good-enough parenting to the next. Whether in Bowie's family or anyone else's, this repeating pattern is a tragedy but there isn't anyone to blame for it.

But hang on, you may be thinking, doesn't there have to be some blame at some point? If we go back far enough won't we find the person who *started* this repeating pattern? Isn't there at some point in the family an original bad or evil person who deliberately hurt their children? Not necessarily. More likely the damage begins through misfortune or simple circumstance. Perhaps a father who never returned from a war, or a mother who died in childbirth. And the consequent sense of abandonment in their child will then be handed down from generation to generation.

This is an important perspective because when we think about unmet childhood needs – which we are about to – it can be natural to blame our parents or other caregivers. And it's helpful (to us) not to do this. Let's work on the basis that the vast majority of parents are well intentioned. They do their best, but perhaps their best has been limited – in some cases severely limited – by their own education, their own experience, their own childhood.

THE LIFE LESSON: HONOUR YOUR UNMET NEEDS

None of us has 'the perfect childhood'. When our childhood needs are not met, we carry those unmet needs into adulthood and they shape our character and our behaviour, sometimes sabotaging our relationships, our career or other aspects of our life. As we continue to develop and grow as human beings, it's important to acknowledge our deepest needs and understand how they trigger 'attachment' – the emotional charge that Buddhism says lies behind much of our mental anguish.

At an early point in his Buddhist studies, the young David Jones will have encountered the four Noble Truths – the cornerstone of Buddhist philosophy. The first Noble Truth states that 'life is suffering'. The second Noble Truth states that 'the cause of suffering is attachment'.

I would hazard a guess that these two sentences have done a very good job of putting many people off Buddhism before they can even discover what it is.

The first Noble Truth sounds decidedly grim, and the second Noble Truth sounds completely unfathomable. Attachment? Attachment to what? Surely it can't be saying you're not supposed to grow attached to your partner or to your children... can it? Are we not supposed to care about other people?

What are the first two Noble Truths really trying to say? Some Buddhist scholars and contemporary teachers acknowledge that the traditional translations are both unhelpful and possibly even inaccurate. Some believe that 'suffering' should be translated as 'dissatisfaction'; others say that the 'life is' construction – suggesting that *all* life is suffering – is too extreme.

The first Noble Truth should perhaps say something more along the lines of 'there's a lot of dissatisfaction in our lives'. It's not as catchy as 'life is suffering', but I think many of us will be able to agree with it.

SO WHAT IS THIS 'ATTACHMENT' THAT BUDDHISTS THINK CAUSES OUR SUFFERING?

Some modern interpreters are also not entirely convinced by the word 'attachment'. However, after 2500 years of trying, nobody has really come up with a better word. Some suggest 'craving' or 'clinging'; they're helpful, but each only suggests a *part* of what the Buddha was talking about. Frankly the idea is so complex that there just isn't a single word that effectively communicates everything that 'attachment' is supposed to convey.

The exact meaning of 'attachment' is both complicated and debatable – as you might expect of a teaching that was first given orally 2500 years ago, then written down by others some time later in one language, Pali, then translated into other languages, including Tibetan, and finally translated into English in a very different time and culture.

However, the way attachment is taught today seems to encompass three closely connected things.

1. *Clinging*: One aspect of attachment is that we desire to hold on to things. Yet they are inevitably transient in nature (another key tenet of Buddhism – one that Bowie embraced wholeheartedly – is that everything is impermanent) so 'suffering' arises when we lose them or due to our fear that we will lose them some day.
2. *Craving*: We believe that acquiring or keeping certain things will make us happy. The 'suffering' arises when they fail to do so.
3. *Pushing away*: We also believe that pushing other things away, or avoiding them in some way, will make us happy. Again, the 'suffering' arises when this turns out not to be the case. This aversion is, in a sense, the opposite of attachment – but it is, in fact, driven by the same forces.

Perhaps the 'craving' variant is the easiest to understand. We have all experienced moments in our life when we believed that acquiring something was going to make us happy, only to find that – while it may give a fleeting pleasure – it doesn't really live up to our expectations. For example:

That dream holiday. You arrive and think 'what a glorious view'. Ten minutes later you notice yourself thinking, 'Well, I've seen the view now.' Half an hour later you realize, 'I'm bored now.'

That promotion. In the years that you desperately wanted it, all you could think about was what you would do with the extra money. Now that you've got it, the money doesn't seem to go very far, and what really preoccupies you is the added responsibility and stress.

That wonderful new phone. You had to have it. But after a couple of days the main thing you notice about it is its annoyingly short battery life.

Even if something new isn't disappointing, within a remarkably small amount of time the innovation that we thought would be life-changing can be taken for granted. So you don't ever think of it with pleasure, although if you lose it, you become miserable.

When was the last time you took five minutes to simply smile with pleasure at the wonder of wi-fi? Probably never. But just how bad do you feel when it goes down? If someone had explained what today's Internet would offer to you twenty-five years ago you would have considered it an extraordinary, wondrous miracle. Now it's just there. Until it isn't and you are sent into a paroxysm of rage and disbelief: how can the world be *so unfair*?

This perennial human trait was once brought vividly to life by an acquaintance who was a high-powered and very highly paid salesperson. All his life he had dreamed of owning a Ferrari. And finally, one day, when he hit a sales target that triggered a huge bonus, he got one. It was delivered to his office and he proudly drove it home, revelling in his dream come true. But after twenty minutes, he phoned his wife:

> 'It's stopped working,' he said dismally.
>
> 'The car's broken down?' she asked incredulously.
>
> 'No, no, it's not broken down. But it's stopped *working*. The thing I bought it for – it doesn't do it any more. When I got in it, it made me feel special, just like I thought it would. But the specialness has worn off already. Now I'm just driving a nice car.'

I won't expect any readers to feel any sympathy for a man who can afford a Ferrari. However, the fact that a car costing a quarter of a million pounds could provide only twenty minutes' worth of 'specialness' shows just how completely wrong our expectations of pleasure can be.

We go through our lives (at whatever income level) feeling slightly dissatisfied, feeling that there is something slightly better out there, something that will make us a much happier person, something that will make our lives complete. In reality, everything we think might do it, ultimately disappoints. It might bring us short-term pleasure, but it doesn't fundamentally make us a happier person. It doesn't sort our lives out for us.

And that's the lucky ones – whose life is essentially OK in the first place. The less lucky ones are going through the same process but on another level: living with a severe or acute problem – anxiety, depression, the constant nagging feeling that they are in some way not good enough – but believing there is something out there that can fix them, cure them, dull the pain, make them feel normal. They too are met with continuing disappointment.

'ATTACHMENT' IS CAUSED BY UNREALISTIC EXPECTATIONS

In all the different variants of attachment, the one constant is a fundamental disconnect with reality. Again and again, we seem to misunderstand how life works, miscalculate the effect some new thing or new relationship will have. We have unrealistic expectations. And however many times we go through the process:

1. anticipation of the thing
2. building up expectations
3. arrival of the thing
4. failure of the thing to meet our expectations

we continue to make the same miscalculation time after time, building up those unrealistic expectations anew, holding out hope that the *next* thing will really be the one that makes our life complete.

If you don't have enough money to pay your bills, then having a pay rise that allows you to pay your bills increases happiness. But research shows that, after that, the incremental effect of more money on happiness is negligible – and that any rise in income over $75,000 a year will cause *absolutely no increase in happiness at all.* So why are so many people working themselves into an early grave to get a huge salary or an astronomical bonus? They believe it will make them happier, but it won't.

We just can't stop ourselves. In the face of all the evidence, our attachment continues.

If we start examining the original Buddhist texts, we encounter the Pali word *tanha*, which is usually translated as 'attachment', but we find that the texts also discuss the *origins* of this clinging. And here we encounter *upanada*, a Pali word that can be translated as 'fuel', 'cause' or 'the means for keeping an active process energized'. And this is what *really* matters to us: what is the fuel that drives the 'clinging' and 'craving' that makes us unhappy? What is the reason for our unreasonable expectations? Why do we ask more of a new thing or a new relationship than it can possibly give?

OUR UNREALISTIC EXPECTATIONS ARE IN TURN FUELLED BY OUR UNMET CHILDHOOD NEEDS

The answer is complex. Part of the answer lies in the survival instincts that have been hardwired into us by evolution, but another part of the answer lies in our upbringing. These false expectations arise from the fact that we routinely expect things in the present day to meet needs that derive from our past. We're expecting them to give more than they can possibly give because we *need* more from them than they can possibly give. We need them to meet the unmet needs of our childhood – to fill the gaps that we have carried around perhaps for decades.

This behaviour of constantly expecting or hoping that things in the present day will meet our needs from the past is – fairly obviously – doomed to failure. Hence the 'suffering'.

Worse, while this strategy fails to deliver what we hope for, it also causes us more harm in the present. Expecting people to meet the needs of our past can damage or completely sabotage our present-day relationships. Expecting things to meet the needs of our past can lead to addictions and other overtly self-damaging behaviours above and beyond the routine disappointments we have discussed already. If we have an especially strong need to compensate for unmet needs, this can be a trigger for disconnection and depression as life relentlessly seems to let us down.

We may not be conscious of the fact that we are seeking to meet our unmet childhood needs, but I have found in my coaching that people only need a few minutes' quiet reflection (not years of therapy) to notice these patterns of behaviour and make links to their childhood.

Understanding these links can lead to:

- *better relationships in the present day* – because you no longer burden people with meeting needs they cannot possibly meet.
- *more enjoyment from material things* – because your appreciation of what they *do* give you is untainted by the disappointment at their failure to meet your unrealistic expectations.
- *wiser decision-making* – because you can better understand the real intentions of others (rather than the emotionally charged effect their words and actions might have on you when they echo childhood scenarios).

SO HOW LIKELY IS IT THAT YOU ARE CARRYING AROUND UNMET CHILDHOOD NEEDS?

There is a pattern of conversation that has occurred in my coaching sessions with several different clients. It goes something like this. We identify a moment when the client has had an extreme overreaction to an event. They acknowledge that it was an extreme overreaction, and start to question why they behaved in this way. They remember other occasions when a similar scenario has played out. We look for causes in the present day but find none. The conversation then continues along these lines:

> Me: Can I ask you about your childhood?
>
> Client: OK.
>
> Me: How would you describe your childhood?
>
> Client: It was fine.
>
> Me: Can you elaborate on that? What do you mean when you say 'fine'?
>
> Client: Well… I wasn't sexually abused or anything like that.
>
> *Sometimes there's a different variant:*
>
> Client: Well… nobody hit me.

This is, frankly, a very low benchmark for deciding that your childhood was 'fine'. These conversations tend to proceed with the client realizing that actually they *are* carrying some unhappiness from their childhood. However, they don't think they should talk about it – and also don't think they deserve any sympathy or compassion for it – because 'other people had it much worse'.

The fact that we are all much more aware of child abuse these days – that victims are much more likely to be believed and that offenders are being punished – is a huge step forward. But it seems to have also brought about this less wonderful side effect: that people who were not physically hurt or abused feel their emotional injuries are not worth bothering about because, comparatively speaking, they 'got off lightly'.

So, let's be clear: you do not have to have had a horrific childhood for you to carry some unmet childhood needs into adulthood. And the fact that 'other people have had it much worse' is no reason not to:

- allow yourself to acknowledge these needs
- offer yourself some kindness and compassion for what you have been through
- do some work now that will help to soothe and heal you.

Sometimes when I'm training groups in emotional intelligence and we're looking at factors that might hinder someone's ability to recognize or express emotions, I will put up a slide showing a list of things that parents might say that could limit their children's ability to feel or communicate their emotions properly. Some of them are quite subtle, but I also put up the classic: 'Stop crying or I'll give you something to cry about.'

When I first began training, I put this slide up in the certain knowledge that we would all be able to discuss it as a sentence that was obviously damaging and that no one in the room would dream of uttering. It was there simply as a marker for how bad things could get. So I was slightly surprised and a little shocked to discover how often the people I was training would say, 'Oh, I say that to my kid.'

When this occurs, there is typically then a pause before they add: 'because that's what my dad/mum used to say to me.'

Another pause and then: 'I won't say it again.'

Often, this is met by murmurs of agreement from around the room. Yes, I've said that too. I didn't mean it. And now that it's written out there on the slide I can see how ridiculous it is and how wrong it is, *but I did say it.*

It's a real lightbulb moment.

Once it's up there on the slide and we're talking about it, everyone can see how cruel the sentence is and that the message it conveys is: 'If you are sad, you will be punished,' which is effectively saying: 'Don't have that feeling. That feeling is bad. You are bad for having feelings.'

It's a potentially damaging lesson to give to anyone, but I think the fact that it remains so widespread illustrates just how easily something gets passed from one generation to the next without being questioned. 'If my parents said it to me,' the logic goes, 'then it's normal parenting and I can say it to my kid. I won't think about what effect it might have on my child because surely if it was a bad thing my parent wouldn't have said it to me in the first place.'

In this way, casual cruelty gets so easily normalized. And the child who hears that phrase (often repeatedly) will carry an unmet childhood need to be heard and understood, a need to express sadness and have their sorrow recognized, and a need for some kindness and compassion.

And when, twenty or thirty years later, their boss says: 'Don't come whining to me about the deadline – just get it done,' they won't leave their boss's office merely thinking 'That wasn't very good people management'; the boss's comment will have an added *emotional charge*, because it echoes the original parental comment. The original unmet need has been unmet again.

And if, on the way home from work, the person who is not allowed to be sad or to complain about an unfair deadline decides 'I need a holiday', that holiday will be expected not just to be a pleasant break; it will be expected to heal the sadness underlying the unmet need. Which it can't. Leading to more disappointment.

HOW CAN WE KNOW WHETHER WE HAVE UNMET CHILDHOOD NEEDS?

This idea of an emotional charge is important. When the Buddhist nun Pema Chödrön teaches about attachment she typically focuses not on clinging, craving or pushing away at all, but on this emotional charge itself. Chödrön's interpretation is interesting to us for two reasons: first because she is a brilliant communicator, and highly skilled at explaining the arcane aspects of Buddhism in clear, simple language that anyone can understand; and second because Chödrön shared two teachers with Bowie.

In the early 1970s Pema Chödrön met Chime Rinpoche at a retreat in the French Alps. He agreed to become her teacher and she began to study with him in London. In 1974, she became a nun under his supervision, and then accepted his advice that she should continue her studies under Chögyam Trungpa Rinpoche, who was her main teacher until his death in 1987. Two major formative influences on Chödrön's interpretation of Buddhism are the men who gave Bowie his direction.

Chödrön chooses to explain attachment not as an abstract concept but by focusing on the effect it has on you. She describes it as those moments when you 'get hooked':

> Somebody says a mean word to you and then something in you tightens – that's the *shenpa* [Tibetan for 'attachment']. Then it starts to spiral into low self-esteem, or blaming them, or anger at them, denigrating yourself. And maybe if you have strong addictions, you just go right for your addiction to cover over the bad feeling that arose when that person said that mean word to you.

We can identify when our unmet childhood needs have been triggered by looking out for Chödrön's version of attachment: that feeling of being hooked, that moment when we sense an exaggerated emotional charge.

How might this reveal itself in everyday life? There's a good chance you're carrying some unmet childhood needs if:

- you regularly find yourself overreacting to situations (on reflection, in the cold light of day, you can look back and think maybe you were a little too angry, too sad, too frightened; or perhaps a friend or colleague tells you to chill out, or suggests you have things a little out of proportion)
- your 'inner critic' often gets very loud (in your head, or maybe even out loud, you speak very harshly to yourself – criticizing yourself for tiny 'mistakes')
- you are very quick to blame others when something goes wrong
- you dread visits to your parents' house or to childhood haunts
- you feel inexplicably guilty every time you walk past a policeman (or generally feel intimidated by authority figures)
- you often have something to contribute to conversations or meetings, but hold back because you think no one really wants to hear from you.

We began this section with the first two Noble Truths, and have puzzled our way through the frankly confusing second one, teasing out the (many and varied) interpretations of 'attachment'. In essence, it comes down to a fundamental miscalculation, misunderstanding or exaggeration of the situation we are in today because of an emotional charge from our past – caused (at least in part) by our unmet childhood needs.

This misunderstanding can take the form of:

- placing unreasonable expectations on people or things (leading to subsequent disappointment)
- placing exaggerated (negative) meaning on events and comments (leading to feeling hurt, frustrated, sad or angry).

But we can do something about this. That's where the other two Noble Truths come in. The third Noble Truth promises that there can be an end to this suffering. The fourth Noble Truth shows us the path to achieve that. Not all of the path is relevant today: you're almost certainly not going to 'adopt the life of a religious mendicant'. The parts of it that make most sense in our modern world are contained in the journey of self-discovery that we began in Chapter 1. So let's continue with it now, and address the unmet needs that trigger attachment and thereby underpin much of the mental anguish in our lives.

YOUR PATH

Before plotting your path into the future, it's important to establish your starting point by looking back to discover how you became who you are today. This process will include identifying and honouring your unmet needs; to balance this, you will also identify and own your strengths.

Every one of the comic-book superheroes who dominate film screens these days has an origin story. And so do you.

Every one of those superheroes was forged through a mixture of triumph and adversity. And so were you.

The creators of those superheroes know exactly how important the origin stories are to the characters. Your origin story is just as important to you. It's important that you know it – and claim it.

As you look closely at the people and events that shaped and influenced you, you will be better able to answer Chime Rinpoche's first two questions:

> Who are you?
>
> Where are you?

Exercise: Identifying unmet childhood needs

How can we identify our unmet childhood needs? Fortunately, life has provided an extremely clear and helpful set of signposts that we can use to identify our unmet needs: our feelings. In particular, the feelings we might usually describe as 'difficult' or 'negative'.

Anger, sadness, frustration and fear often occur when the needs that really matter to us – the ones that weren't met in our childhood – are unmet in the present day. More precisely, it is when these feelings occur to an exaggerated extent – out of proportion to what has triggered them – that we can be reasonably sure they are pointing to an unmet childhood need.

If we work hard on a report at work and give it to our boss, and our boss doesn't read it, we are entitled to feel a bit frustrated. But the important point is that we are entitled to feel *a bit* frustrated.

These things happen at work. Our boss may be busy. They may be very keen to read our report, they may value the work that they know we have put into it, but they may simply have no time in their schedule to sit and read it properly. They'll get round to it, eventually, but not as quickly as you would like. So yes, it's entirely understandable that you would be a bit frustrated.

However, if you find yourself waking up at 3 a.m., lying awake for two hours obsessing about the fact that your boss still hasn't read your report and wondering how they dare to disrespect you in this way, this is an out-of-proportion response to your boss's poor time management. You should therefore ask yourself: does this situation bear any resemblance to situations I experienced when I was younger?

Perhaps it does. Perhaps there was a moment when you rushed to tell your father about a great mark you got for some work at school, only to be told 'Daddy's busy now.' Or perhaps – like Bowie – you can remember as a child getting out your paints, only for a parent to say: 'Don't make a mess.'

It's not a terrible thing for a parent to say. In fact, it's quite understandable. But if – as with Peggy – it is the *only* thing they say when you get your paints out, it can hurt. If there is no excitement about what you might be about to create, no desire to see the finished object, no pride in hanging it on the fridge – if your need for appreciation and encouragement is completely ignored – then, at any point in the future when you have the same need and it once again goes unmet, it will hurt again.

Knowing that our emotions can signpost our unmet needs, especially those moments when we seem to have overreacted emotionally to what's happening around us, we can use the following table to start to identify what our unmet childhood needs are.

This isn't an exercise to do in a hurry. Find a private space and a time when you won't have to rush off to the next thing.

We've got limited space in the pages of the book, so I would suggest drawing this table out on a very large piece of paper and giving yourself time and space to go through the process as many times as you can.

Cast your mind back over the past few days to moments when you have experienced what you might consider to be 'negative emotions' – anger, sadness, frustration, fear – particularly thinking of occasions when, on reflection, you might have overreacted or when your emotions might have made you say something you later regretted. (If you don't have any moments from the last few days, then cast your mind back further. It really doesn't matter how old the memories are.) Then, with each memory in turn, go through the seven questions on the table.

	Event 1	Event 2	Event 3	Event 4
What did I feel? (And what else?)				
What happened immediately before?				
What else happened before that?				
How often do I react like this?				
Do I consider this feeling my friend or foe?				
If this feeling was my friend, what was it trying to tell me?				
What was my unmet need?				

What did I feel? (And what else?) Describe the feeling in as much detail as you can. If there were secondary feelings detail those as well.

What happened immediately before? What triggered this feeling? What was the event or comment, or action that immediately preceded the feeling?

What else happened before that? Were there any other contributing circumstances that may have added to the strength of the feeling? Were you reacting to one event – or a series of events?

How often do I react like this? Thinking back, how often would you say you react in this way?

Do I consider this feeling my friend or foe? In this situation did you consider this emotion to be helping you, or hindering you? Did it make you do or say anything you later regretted? If the answer is 'neither' that's perfectly OK.

If this feeling was my friend, what was it trying to tell me? Whatever your answer to the previous question, now consider that this emotion was trying to help you by giving you important information. What might it have been telling you?

What was my unmet need? Finally, ask yourself, what could be the unmet need from earlier in your life that lay behind your emotional reaction?

To help you answer this last question, here is a list of typical human needs. (This list comes from the Centre for Nonviolent Communication. You can find out a lot more about nonviolent communication and the work they do at their website www.cnvc.org.) As you can see, there are quite a few.

CONNECTION
acceptance
affection
appreciation
belonging
cooperation
communication
closeness
community
companionship
compassion
consideration
consistency
empathy
inclusion
intimacy
love
mutuality
nurturing
respect/self-respect
safety
security
stability
support
to know and be known
to see and be seen
to understand and be understood
trust
warmth

PHYSICAL WELL-BEING
air
food
movement/exercise
rest/sleep
sexual expression
safety
shelter
touch
water

HONESTY
authenticity
integrity
presence

PLAY
joy
humour

PEACE
beauty
communion
ease
equality
harmony
inspiration
order

AUTONOMY
choice
freedom
independence
space
spontaneity

MEANING
awareness
celebration of life
challenge
clarity
competence
consciousness
contribution
creativity
discovery
efficacy
effectiveness
growth
hope
learning
mourning
participation
purpose
self-expression
stimulation
to matter
understanding

As you go through these questions again for more memories, you may notice that some themes emerge. If you spot repeated patterns, this is likely to indicate a particularly powerful unmet need.

Remember, our intention is to not blame anyone for this. As these unmet needs emerge, if you feel angry remember that your anger is valid and you are entitled to feel it. But, if at all possible, let your anger be 'anger because' not 'anger at'. Anger *because* your needs were unmet, not anger *at* the person who failed to meet your needs. As we discussed earlier in the chapter, that person may have been well intentioned and simply limited in their ability to meet your needs by circumstance or their own personal history.

A strategy for healing

Having identified each unmet need, work through these steps to help yourself heal.

1. *Honour your unmet needs.* A meditation to help you do this is outlined in the exercise below.
2. *Appreciate those moments when your needs are met.* As you become aware of your unmet childhood needs, through reviewing the times when they haven't been met, also start to look out for times when those needs *are* met, and note who in your life meets them. Make a point of expressing your gratitude to these people. You don't have to say 'thank you for meeting my unmet childhood need' (not everyone would understand or appreciate what you mean by that); you can simply send an email that says something like 'thanks for your

prompt reply; getting your feedback so quickly really made a difference to the success of the project'.

3. *Look for practical ways to get your needs met in the present day.* You may want to spend less time with people you identify as failing to meet your needs, and more time with those who do. As you become more aware of your needs, you will also be able to find ways to express them calmly, clearly and concisely to others in language that is appropriate to the present-day situation.

4. *Accept that we won't be able to fully meet all our unmet childhood needs in the present day.* Know that sometimes your needs won't be met but now you have a way of dealing with this: the meditation outlined in the following exercise.

Exercise: Honour your unmet childhood needs

As you surface unmet childhood needs, use this meditation to give yourself care and healing.

We have all had the experience of a friend who comes to us with a problem. We listen and we very quickly see a brilliant solution to their problem. So we share it with them. Oddly, however, they seem entirely unimpressed with our brilliant solution. If anything, they seem a bit annoyed. They didn't want us to *fix* anything. They just wanted us to be there to listen. They wanted our kind, caring, undivided attention.

This is the attitude that we will bring to this meditation. We're not trying to fix anything. Fixing isn't what is needed. We just need to be there. In this case we're not there for a friend but for our self, offering our self the kind, caring, undivided attention it needs.

Don't rush this. If you come to this meditation with any sense of resentment at having to spend this time with your self, or any sense that you really ought to be doing something else, you will not be able to be truly caring and healing for your self. Make sure you can set the time aside first before starting.

This intention to just be there for our self is all that really matters in this meditation. Finding and naming unmet needs is not a precise science, and this exercise is not a forensic investigation. It is a gentle re-parenting.

For the purposes of explaining the meditation, I will take the example of Bowie and the childhood paints. When this is retriggered, what is the unmet childhood need? Looking through the list, we might say 'appreciation' or perhaps 'to be seen' – as a whole person, not just something that might cause a mess. You will, of course, substitute your own unmet need.

Begin the meditation as we did the meditations in Chapter 1. Sit in a state of relaxed alertness, close your eyes and focus on your breath. Get in touch with the rhythm of the in breath and the out breath.

When thoughts arise, let them go and return your focus to the breath.

Allow your breathing to become a little bit slower, a little bit deeper, with a long relaxed out breath.

Once you are fully attuned to the rhythm of the breath, state the unmet need to yourself in any language that makes sense to you: 'I would like to be appreciated' or 'I need to be seen for who I am.' Allow yourself the feelings that this thought provokes in you.

Start to scan slowly through your body to find where these feelings resonate. Start at the head and work down. Check in with each part of your body until you find the place where this need lies.

It may be that your throat has tightened, or there is a heaviness in your chest; your stomach might feel woozy or your shoulders might have tensed. You might be gritting your teeth, or your hands may have formed into fists. Or you may have some other reaction. Just scan through your body until you find it.

When you find it, simply stay with it. Place your focus on the part of your body that has reacted to the need, and simply stay with it. As you do so, keep breathing slowly and steadily, with a long relaxed out breath.

You are not trying to get rid of this feeling. You are allowing it to be just as it is.

You are not trying to figure out what's going on or to understand why you feel this way. All you're doing is offering yourself some care and attention.

Notice if the feeling stays the same or changes (without trying to change it). Notice if it moves around your body. Whatever arises, simply stay with it.

Allow yourself a few minutes of just being with what is.

Then gently and gradually return your focus to your breath. As you focus on the breath, bring a sense of letting go to each out breath. Audibly sighing slightly as you breathe out can help.

After a few of these deep 'letting go' breaths, gently open your eyes.

Exercise: Owning your strengths

In a 1999 BT webchat, Bowie said this of his early career: 'I had incredibly low self-esteem, which drove me to constantly try to improve what I was doing, and still I had this constant feeling of failure. I was constantly *constantly* – about to give up hope with regard to what I was doing.' Yet this was a man who created one of the greatest artistic bodies of work of the past hundred years. Our self-perception can be *so* wrong.

Even when we lack confidence, even when we doubt ourselves, the reality is usually that we have many strengths and fine qualities. Even when we feel quite alone, we may in fact have a support network around us.

Some people can be reluctant to claim their strengths, but it will help us on our journey of self-discovery to acknowledge our positive qualities, and to also acknowledge our support network.

Work your way through the following questions. (If you find the exercise helpful, you can work through the questions several times, each time focusing on a different challenge in your life.)

Remember a time when you faced a situation that you found difficult or challenging but that you nevertheless dealt with (maybe not 100 per cent successfully, but you coped – you got through it). Recall what happened, using these questions as prompts.

1. What did you want to achieve?
2. What actually happened?
3. What were the specific challenges you faced (or why did you find this situation difficult)?
4. What 'negative' feelings and/or self-critical thoughts do you remember having?
5. Did you ask for help?
6. If so, who helped you?
7. Why did you choose that particular person (or those people)? What qualities do they have?
8. What were your own personal qualities that helped you through the situation?
9. With hindsight, what might you have done differently? (No beating yourself up here; we can all do better with the benefit of hindsight.)
10. If someone else was facing a similar situation now, what advice would you give them? And what help could you offer them?

After you've finished, look back at your answers to questions 8, 9 and 10. Think about the qualities you have identified here, the learnings you gained, and the way you would now be able to help someone else.

When you face future tough challenges, check back through these points and work out how you can apply these strengths, learnings and advice to the new situation.

Work through this exercise several times if possible (using different challenges from your past) to build up your list of strengths and learnings.

Exercise: Who influences you?

Complete these sentences. Add as much detail or explanation as you like. Try to be as specific as possible when saying what lesson you learned and when it comes in useful

The person who influences me most in my life is...

The most important lesson I learned from them was...

A time when this came in really useful was...

If the person you have named above is a family member, now answer all three questions again about someone who is not related to you.

A person who influences me greatly in my life is...

The most important lesson I learned from them was...

It's come in really useful when...

Exercise: Who helps you?

Thinking not about the past but about the present day, answer these questions.

1. Who can you turn to for help? (name as many as you like)
2. What positive qualities do they possess that makes them a great person to go to for support?
3. If someone turns to you for support, what positive qualities do you possess that will help you support them?
4. How do you use these positive qualities to support yourself?
5. How else could you use them on your own behalf?

Review your answers to the questions in the last two exercises. Look at the strengths you have detected and the support you have identified. Whenever you meet new challenges, come back to these questionnaires, review them and see how you can apply these strengths and call on this support to help you in the new situation.

If you feel it is appropriate, consider contacting the people you identified who influence you and help you and telling them that you've just been through this exercise and that you identify them as someone who is very important in your life. Let them know how they have helped you and thank them. If any of them are no longer alive, just hold them in your thoughts for a few minutes.

Your path: Going forward

After you've been through the exercises above, try the following.

1. Continue to meditate regularly (as in Chapter 1, focusing on your breath but noticing thoughts and judgements) for three minutes every day. If you can do it for longer, fantastic. But three minutes is enough for you to notice your mind wandering into thought and judgement, and to gently bring it back to the breath. As you do this you are strengthening a valuable skill that will have applications throughout this book.

2. Start to notice when people around you overreact to situations. Ponder what the unmet need driving this could be. What need could have been unmet in the present situation? (Don't tell them. This is about you developing the skill of noticing unmet needs, not intervening in their life.)

3. Think about Chime Rinpoche's first two questions:

   Who are you?
   Where are you?

   What have you taken out of these exercises that helps you to answer those questions more fully?

4. Ask yourself this question: 'Who would I be without my unmet childhood needs?' As a thought experiment, live with that question for a week.

CHAPTER 3: MASKS

The life lesson: Dismantle the defences that hold you back

Crazy? Sane? Man? Woman? Robot?

(US talk-show host Dick Cavett introducing Bowie, 1974)

That fucker [Ziggy Stardust] would not leave me alone for years… my whole personality was affected… it became very dangerous. I really did have doubts about my sanity… I think I put myself very dangerously near the line.

(David Bowie in an interview with Allan Jones, Melody Maker*, 1977)*

All your rebirths could ultimately make you sick… a chameleon, a caricature, one prone to changing colours, a crawling shimmering lizard.

(Carl Jung, The Red Book*)*

BOWIE'S PATH

To the rest of the world, the characters Bowie devised – like Ziggy Stardust – were fabulous artistic creations. But for Bowie, as he later came to realize, they were psychological defences that he constructed to avoid confronting the aspects of reality he didn't like.

Long before he walked into the Buddhist Society and met Chime Rinpoche, Bowie had another brilliant teacher: his half-brother, Terry Burns. For most of his adult life Bowie would be the coolest man on the planet, but as a young child he put Terry on that particular pedestal.

As a 1970s superstar, Bowie took great pleasure in introducing his legion of fans to brilliant but lesser-known artists (such as the Velvet Underground and Iggy Pop). He was doing for his public exactly what Terry had done for him fifteen years earlier.

Terry was ten years older than David, and he fired young David's imagination by introducing him to R&B, science fiction, modern jazz, and to the writing of the Beat Generation: Jack Kerouac, Allen Ginsberg, Gregory Corso, Lawrence Ferlinghetti, William Burroughs and John Clellon Holmes.

There is a 1962 edition of Jack Kerouac's novel *The Dharma Bums* with a wonderfully pulpy cover. The cover line reads

'Fighting, drinking, scorning convention, making wild love – zany antics of America's young Beats in their mad search for kicks' and below this blatant attempt to lure a large audience to a left-field novel is the considered verdict of the usually staid magazine *The Listener*: 'Adds up to one hell of a philosophy of life.'

Well, yes it does, but – presumably to the surprise and maybe disappointment of those attracted by the cover – that philosophy turns out to be Buddhism.

The clue is in the title. *Dharma* is another one of those words that's not easy to translate exactly, but it can refer either to the teachings of the Buddha or to the way one should live in following them. Like 'tao', it is both the code and the path. The characters in the book are as much seekers after truth as they are sensation seekers, and their way of finding the truth is through Buddhism.

Crucially, as well as expanding Bowie's frame of reference way outside of mainstream culture, Terry was also providing a gateway to Buddhism. In this case, Zen Buddhism rather than the Tibetan Buddhism that Bowie went on to study with Chime Rinpoche, but in both variations meditation is at the core of the practice, and Bowie would remain fascinated by Zen as well.

Much later, Bowie acknowledged in an American TV documentary:

> I think that Terry probably gave me the greatest education – serviceable education – I could ever have had. I mean, he just introduced me to the outside things. The first real

> major event for me was when he passed Jack Kerouac's *On the Road* on to me, which really changed my life, and he also introduced me to people like John Coltrane, which is way above my head, but I saw the magic. I caught the enthusiasm for it because of his enthusiasm. I wanted to be kind of like him.

Young David wanted to be like big brother Terry. Until one day he very definitely didn't.

THE RISE OF DAVID AND THE FALL OF TERRY

In 1967 Terry had a major breakdown, hallucinating and hearing voices. Terry had had a history of mental health issues. But now things got significantly worse. He was soon diagnosed with schizophrenia and placed in a psychiatric institution, the Cane Hill asylum.

To begin with, Bowie remained a caring brother to Terry, but over time this attitude changed. Seeing Terry so vividly living out the 'family curse', David dealt with his own fear of mental illness by gradually shutting Terry out of his life. In 1971, when Terry turned up at Haddon Hall, where Bowie – on the cusp of fame – was living with his then-wife Angie and some of the band who would become The Spiders from Mars, Bowie dismissed him with: 'I'm sorry. We're busy.'

It seems extremely harsh, but Bowie was clearly worried that he would suffer the same fate as Terry. He didn't want to think about the 'family curse' but, if Terry was around, he was forced to. So Terry had to go. The fact that he saw Terry's presence as a threat to his own sanity was evident in comments he made to his cousin Kristina later in 1971 when he visited her in New York. Kristina remembers Bowie saying that he couldn't understand 'why he was chosen and Terry was left. He could have been Terry.'

Bowie's dread that it could just as easily be him in the asylum, and his inability to get too close to Terry after this point, was brought vividly to life when he later told a journalist: 'I was never quite sure what real position Terry had in my life, whether Terry was a real person, or whether I was actually referring to another part of me.'

While Bowie rose to fame, Terry's life went in another direction. In 1965 he had told Madeleine Berks, his landlady at the time: 'I've read Freud and I've read Jung and I know exactly where I'm heading.' Berks took the comment to mean that he was going to kill himself.

Meanwhile, Bowie's fear, confusion and guilt surfaced in some of his most powerful songs of the era: 'All the Madmen' on *The Man Who Sold the World* album, 'Changes' and 'The Bewlay Brothers' on *Hunky Dory*, 'Five Years' on *The Rise and Fall of Ziggy Stardust and the Spiders From Mars*. As these songs helped propel Bowie to stardom, it is tempting to be critical of his treatment of Terry. Some biographers have indeed accused him of effectively locking Terry up and throwing away the key. I think to blame Bowie for this is as misguided as it would be to blame Peggy Jones or Margaret Burns for the two men's mental health issues. Everyone in this story is doing the best they can with the limited emotional resources they have.

The proof that Bowie couldn't have cared better for Terry is that over the next few years he showed the same complete lack of care for himself. If Bowie 'locked Terry up and threw away the key', then he was simultaneously doing exactly the same to himself. But whereas Terry was trapped in an asylum, Bowie was trapped inside a self-created monster called Ziggy Stardust.

THE *REAL* RISE AND FALL OF ZIGGY STARDUST

Bowie had read Jung too.

The psychology of Carl Gustav Jung had joined Buddhism as one of the thought traditions that Bowie explored in his life and his work. And, again like Buddhism, Jung's ideas would stay with him throughout his life. Tony Oursler, who directed the extraordinary video for Bowie's 2013 'comeback' single 'Where Are We Now?' (the title of which nods back to Chime Rinpoche's three questions), said that year in an interview with *Le Figaro* that: 'Bowie inhabits Carl Jung's world… reading and speaking of the psychoanalyst with a passion.' In fact, if you want to explore the key concepts of Jungian psychology, Bowie is a perfect case study.

It is Jung's concept of the persona that is most relevant to us here. The persona, according to Jung, is the face we show the world – a mask for our interactions with others. It is not our true self, it is the 'shop window' we put out into the world. Bowie took the concept of the persona and ran with it.

In 1972, Bowie had been trying to make it in the music industry for nine years. He had achieved one hit single ('Space Oddity') but had otherwise been largely ignored. Then he created Ziggy

Stardust and everything changed. Bowie had tried to be a rock star, and failed to be a rock star. So now he decided to simply *act* the role of a rock star. He wrote an album about Ziggy Stardust, a fictional rock star, and began to perform in Ziggy's clothes and make-up.

It was a post-modernist coup d'état. By simply *saying* that he was a rock star, he *became* one. At the peak of the Ziggy era, Bowie had five albums in the UK Top 40 (including reissued versions of three albums that had been virtually ignored by the record-buying public before the creation of Ziggy). Within a few months Bowie had become, without question, the most important figure in UK popular culture since The Beatles. To the outside world it looked like genius. Inside Bowie, however, it quickly became a nightmare.

Jung said we create a persona to project outwards the bits of us that others will find acceptable, allowing us to bury within us the bits that we think they won't find acceptable (because we don't think that they are). Ziggy Stardust allowed Bowie to send the confident version of himself on stage, while the scared, fragmented, vulnerable, emotionally starved and developmentally stunted version of himself stayed locked up underneath.

Jung had taken the word 'persona' from Latin, where it meant the mask worn by an actor in classical drama. In a sense, an acting role is a temporary persona. Bowie saw himself as an actor as well as a singer, and Ziggy was initially an acting role for him. Interviewed in his dressing room during the Ziggy years, he said, 'I believe in my part all the way down the line. I do play it for all its worth. That's part of what Bowie's supposed to be about. I'm an actor.'

And in that last sentence we encounter the first reason why Ziggy became a problem. Bowie is talking about 'Bowie' as a third person because 'Bowie' was already a persona created by David Jones. The persona is supposed to be the acceptable face you show the world, but 'Bowie' had failed to be accepted by enough people. So Jones/Bowie now created *another* persona. Ziggy was a persona on top of a persona.

A few years later, when Bowie was filming *The Man Who Fell to Earth*, the director Nicolas Roeg warned him that sometimes, when an actor finishes a film, the character stays with them. It was a useful warning. For Bowie it came too late; he had already learned this the hard way.

Bowie had decided not to leave Ziggy on stage. Instead, he thought, why not take him to interviews? Why not play Ziggy in front of the press? And then, why not take Ziggy out in public? And then, why stop being Ziggy at all? Initially it seemed like a good idea. It made things simpler, but pretty soon Bowie was – as he later put it – 'lost in Ziggy'. Possibly Bowie had become Ziggy. Or maybe Ziggy had become Bowie. Whatever was going on, Bowie soon came to hate Ziggy as much as his fans loved the character.

When Bowie killed off Ziggy in the summer of 1973 at the height of his fame, it was considered either an inexplicable mistake (how could anyone throw away a character that had generated such success and indeed income?) or another show-business masterstroke (what an extraordinary way to generate even more hype!). While the musicians in his backing band, The Spiders from Mars, were rocked by the decision, Bowie appeared to the outside world to be gliding smoothly on to the next stage in his career. In reality there was nothing smooth about it.

According to biographer Christopher Sandford, Bowie sobbed in an alleyway before the July 1973 show at the Hammersmith Odeon where he 'killed' Ziggy. At one point when his manager screamed 'Where's David?', his guitarist Mick Ronson recalls Bowie answering: 'You tell me.' And then, after his apparently super-cool, artfully staged moment just before the encores when he told the audience that this was 'the last show we'll ever do', he returned to his dressing room and trashed it, also hurting himself in the process. When he emerged observers saw scratches and bruising on his face. Perhaps 'killing off Ziggy' had originally been seen as a clever career ploy but, in this moment, Bowie knew that he had discarded his persona and he was left with... well, what?

As he said several times in his career, 'there is no definitive David Bowie'. As for David Jones, he had no idea at all where that person was. Trying to find David Jones was 'like playing the shell game', he told *Rolling Stone* in 1975. 'Except I've got so many shells I've forgotten what the pea looks like. I wouldn't know it if I found it.'

By the time of that *Rolling Stone* interview he had created (or was developing) several more personas to cover up the parts of himself he didn't like (including his gnawing fear of mental illness): Aladdin Sane, a hybrid of Ziggy, who wore the lightning-bolt make-up that became Bowie's most enduring image; Halloween Jack, who lived in the dystopian future of his

Diamond Dogs album; a 'plastic soul character' who sang his biggest US hit, 'Fame'; and the Thin White Duke, a cold, brutal, proto-dictator with worryingly fascistic tendencies. And as each new persona arrived, Bowie's state of mind worsened until he was alienated, alone, anorexic and addicted – living proof of Jung's assertion that 'All your rebirths could ultimately make you sick.'

Bowie had employed two defensive mechanisms to shield himself from the parts of himself (and his family) that he didn't want to face: his multiple personas and his constant busyness. Initially both defences had worked. As the 1970s wore on, they were both crumbling – doing Bowie far more harm than good.

THE LIFE LESSON: DISMANTLE THE DEFENCES THAT HOLD YOU BACK

We all create defences or 'false refuges' that seem initially attractive and may even work for a while as a means of getting us successfully through life, but over time – instead of protecting us – they add to our suffering.

In 1982, after several unsuccessful suicide attempts, Terry Burns took his own life.

Was Terry's sad death as inevitable as he appeared to be suggesting when he told Madeleine Berks, 'I've read Freud and I've read Jung and I know exactly where I'm heading'? It's a strange comment. It suggests that, if Terry had read Jung, he clearly hadn't *understood* Jung. There is nothing in Jung's work that suggests that mental illness – even schizophrenia – is incurable or that Terry's prognosis would have been one of inevitable, irreversible decline. Quite the opposite.

While conventional psychiatry, at the time Jung was developing his theories, saw patients as victims of an illness, Jung saw them as someone who was ready to grow, to become a more complete human being. Conventional psychiatry wants to reduce suffering (and anyone who has suffered with mental illness will agree that this is a perfectly sensible aim), but Jung believed there was scope to do more than this – that a patient's suffering could be used as a springboard for the patient's growth, and that the exact nature of the suffering – the symptoms displayed – were an indicator of exactly how they needed to grow and how they could grow.

Rather than thinking that something had gone horribly wrong that needed fixing, to Jung mental illness was a sign that you may be stuck on your journey through life, but you didn't have to stay stuck. However ill you were, Jung was convinced that 'schizophrenic disturbances could be treated and cured by psychological means'.

Psychiatry saw the delusions, hallucinations, unusual gestures and speech patterns of schizophrenics as nonsense. Jung saw them as filled with meaning. As he wrote in 1914, 'When we penetrate into the human secrets of our patients, the madness discloses the system upon which it is based, and we recognize insanity to be simply an unusual reaction to emotional problems which are in no wise foreign to ourselves.'

Although Jung was a radical thinker, it seems unlikely that Terry would have failed to understand what he wrote. In the works that he recommended to his younger half-brother, Terry had already shown himself to be bright, inquisitive and extremely open to new ideas. Perhaps we have to conclude that, while Terry may have understood what Jung was saying, his experience had already shown him that the people charged with his care did not. Tragically, it seems that at no point in his time in the asylum did he receive any talking therapy at all.

WHERE JUNG MEETS THE BUDDHA

It would probably be stretching it to say that the Buddha's philosophy and Jung's psychology were the same, but they are extraordinarily close to each other. Given that they were separated by two and a half millennia and existed in such completely different cultures, the two men arrived at eerily similar conclusions about why we suffer and how we can best find our way through life. It's no surprise that someone like Bowie, who was attracted to one, would also immerse themselves in the other.

Here are just a few of the similarities:

1. Both Buddhism and Jungian psychology argue that the way to end suffering, and indeed the true purpose of life, is to find out who you really are. This is the most important work you can do in your time on earth.
2. In Buddhism you follow the eightfold path to an end point, enlightenment – the fullest realization of a human being. In Jung's scheme of things, the process is called individuation, and the end point, again, is to become the most fully realized version of yourself that you can be.
3. This may seem self-centred – even selfish – but both traditions emphasize that it isn't. This work on your self improves all your relationships and makes you a more positive, loving and giving presence in the world. 'You cannot individuate on Everest,' Jung declared.

4. A crucial step on the path to either individuation or enlightenment is to understand that the self that you carry around in the world isn't your real self. On both paths, you must look within to see clearly the illusions and deceptions of normal life, and you must find and integrate your true self.

5. This discovery of the true self will not always be a comfortable process because it will involve stripping away the defences that you have erected to close off parts of your self that you (or others) have in the past deemed unacceptable. You must actively reclaim these parts of your self that you have tried to discard or repress in the past.

6. Learning to stay with uncomfortable feelings is at the heart of both processes. As Jung said (in a line echoed in Bowie's song 'Changes'), 'self-realization requires the psyche to turn round on itself and confront what it produces'.

7. This is not purely (or even primarily) an intellectual pursuit. Jung said those who 'understand with their brains only' would never achieve the transformation. In Buddhism, thoughts are considered in many ways a distraction from the work you need to do.

8. You do not explicitly try to increase happiness, meaning or purpose, but these are the by-products of the work. Striving after the things that you think will lead to happiness is replaced by greater acceptance of things as they are.

9. Although there is a notional end point in both traditions, they share the view that the journey is far more important than the destination.

10. As you continue the work you will get a greater sense of how you are connected to the rest of the world.

11. Although you may have a teacher or a therapist, *you* do the work, you make the decisions, and you take nothing they say as 'the truth', instead increasing your knowledge and understanding through your own direct experience of your inner world.

THE PERSONA: IT'S YOU... BUT IT'S NOT YOU

Point 4 is where things start to get hard to grasp. You're not you? Then who are you? The Buddhist answer to this is complex, and we'll look at it in more detail in Chapter 8. From Jung's point of view, the false self that you carry round in the world is your persona. It is a mask you wear both to create a specific impression on other people and also to conceal the bits of you that you would rather hide. It is essentially a compromise between who you are and who you think society expects you to be.

In Bowie's case, it was made clear to him growing up that emotions were not to be expressed. So his persona was emotion-free. In your case, perhaps you learned growing up that you should always please people, in which case your persona is always very friendly and approachable. Or you may have found little sympathy when you were feeling sad, so your persona is always relentlessly upbeat.

This, from Jung's perspective, is entirely normal human activity. We all do it, and it helps us function in the world. In the natural course of things, there will come a time when the individual no longer wants to – or feels no longer able to – maintain their persona. This is, in popular parlance, the midlife crisis. At this point the healthy person moves further along the journey of individuation, by integrating their persona with the previously hidden aspects of their personality. They thus become a more fully rounded, authentic version of themselves.

That's the normal run of things. But personas can go badly wrong:

if the persona is too heavily weighted towards what you think others want to see, and has little of the real you in it.

if you use the persona not simply to conceal aspects of your personality that you think others won't like, but to try *to get rid of* aspects of your personality that you don't like. 'A man cannot get rid of himself in favour of an artificial personality without punishment,' Jung wrote (by 'punishment' he meant mental health issues).

if you lose sight of the fact that your persona is not you. If you become so identified with your 'image' that you start 'believing your own publicity'.

if your persona is too successful. If your persona becomes richly rewarded – with money, attention, career success, respect, power – you may be drawn to identify too strongly with it.

if we find the thought of dropping our persona and just being our real self (even temporarily) to be frightening or upsetting.

As we saw earlier, Bowie ticked all of these boxes. When you tick even some of them, your persona stops being a useful tool to help you navigate your life, and instead becomes a defence that you are putting up to rigidly protect you from what you perceive to be unwanted aspects of your real self.

DEFENCES: FRIEND OR FOE?

As with our persona, if we use psychological defences occasionally and mindfully they can be a helpful way to get us through the trickier moments in our life. But if they start to dominate us – if we turn to them habitually – they will quickly become a problem. Instead of smoothing our way, they will cause us additional problems, while at the same time sucking all the joy out of our lives.

The defences that we can employ include the following.

Avoidance: Perhaps the most straightforward defence mechanism. You simply avoid the situation that will trigger the unwanted emotions. If you know that speaking in public triggers anxiety in you, then you may choose not to try for the promotion that would put you in a role where you would be expected to present to the board once a quarter. You might be well aware that you are sabotaging yourself by deliberately stopping yourself from chasing a job that you would otherwise like, or you might manage to convince yourself that you never wanted the job anyway, in which case you would also be using…

Denial: We all know this one. It has passed into common usage. Denial is when you simply refuse to accept the reality of the situation – even when it's staring you in the face. In all probability everyone around you can see the facts, but you refuse to. It's also quite possible that someone is telling you that you are 'in denial'. But you won't have it.

Repression: When something is difficult for us to think about or feel, we can sometimes push it down into our unconscious to hide it from ourselves. This is more than simply putting it out of our mind. If an event, feeling or thought is truly repressed we have no idea that it actually happened.

Projection: When you have feelings about yourself that you don't like, you can instead apply them to one or more of the people around you. So if you are lazy but it's important to your self-image to see yourself as an efficient, hard-working, gets-things-done kind of person, then you will tend to blame those around you for screwing things up due to *their* laziness. In extreme cases you attribute all positive qualities to yourself and attribute all negative qualities to someone else (or to another group of people).

Displacement: This occurs when, for example, one person makes you angry but you take the anger out on someone else instead. This may happen because you feel unable to be angry with the first person (perhaps they are your boss), but feel OK about being angry at the second person (somebody less powerful).

Splitting: In his essay 'The Crack-Up', F. Scott Fitzgerald wrote, 'the test of a first-rate intelligence is the ability to hold two opposed ideas in the mind at the same time, and still retain the ability to function.' It's a widely quoted idea and it has much truth in it – especially if we insert the word 'emotional' in front of the word 'intelligence'. People with low emotional intelligence can find ambiguity and uncertainty quite difficult to deal with. To avoid having to deal with it they use splitting: instead of dealing with the complexities of a situation, they opt to simply see only one side of the argument. They see everything as black and white. There are no grey areas, and there is no scope for debate or compromise.

Sublimation: When we sublimate, we reapply our unwanted feelings into an area where they are more socially acceptable. When another motorist cuts in front of us we take the rage that this creates in us to the gym, where we 'punish' the equipment (possibly while fantasizing about what we would like to do to the motorist).

Busyness and distraction: One of the simplest ways to avoid unwanted thoughts and feelings, anxiety or fear is to throw yourself into some activity or another – especially one that is complicated or engaging enough to demand your full attention.

There are many other psychological defences, but that will do to be going on with.

All of them can be used in a positive way. For example, when a loved one dies, we will not be able to deal with all the grief in one go; a certain judicious use of denial and a bit of busyness can help us to cope. However, all defences are potentially problematic if we over-use them.

Denial and repression may work in the short term but, as the saying goes, 'what we resist persists'. Over the long term the feelings we are trying to avoid will resurface. And they tend to come back stronger than before.

Projection and displacement can damage your relationships, as you routinely blame people for things that aren't their fault, or treat them badly for no reason. Taken to the extreme, projection and displacement can be the underlying cause of bigotry and racism.

The negative consequences of splitting are, unfortunately, all too visible in our culture at the moment. You only have to look at social media discussions of major political issues to see how poisonous splitting can become. When you split, you don't just favour one side of an argument, you believe you are totally right and the other side is totally wrong. Issues like Brexit or personalities like Donald Trump have shown us how quickly that can spiral into believing that the other side is 'bad' or maybe even 'evil'. To understand why splitting can easily become an unhealthy defence, just try to imagine one of those social media battles being waged in your brain.

Sublimation is generally considered one of the most mature or least harmful defences. After all, if you're taking your anger out on a punch bag, who's actually getting damaged? Well, in fact, you are. Because every time you do that, you are strengthening the connection in your brain between anger and aggression, and therefore making it even harder for you to deal with anger in a healthier way next time it arises.

So, in Jungian terms, an emotionally healthy person has a persona but is – to some degree – aware that this is them 'putting their best self on show', and stays in touch with the less lovely parts of themselves that reside in their self. Their persona and their self never drift too far away from each other.

Equally, a healthy person will use defences to help them navigate tricky moments in life, but will do so sparingly and with some understanding of what they are doing. Faced with difficult emotions, they might use a defence to avoid them but they are saying: 'I can't deal with this *now*,' not: 'I'm *never* going to deal with this.'

But if we identify entirely with our persona or if we over-use our defences, they just can't cope. And then, ironically, our attempts to save ourselves from suffering will cause us suffering. Our repression and denial may surface as tensions in the body, psychosomatic symptoms, anxieties and phobias; our projection, displacement and splitting may surface as anger, judging and obsessing.

As you use defences to limit the amount of negative feelings you experience, the inevitable consequence is that you also limit your ability to experience your positive feelings. Unfortunately, our defences aren't highly trained snipers. They can't pick out the exact target they're looking for. They also cause a lot of collateral damage, taking out many of our good feelings along with the bad ones. As a result, our life can become contracted, difficult and devoid of joy.

YOUR PATH

The next stage on our journey of self-discovery is to gradually reduce the number of defences we use and the amount of time we spend using them. Then – as we go forward – we can notice our defences as they arise, and ensure that we choose to use them sparingly and appropriately.

The fact that the defences we put in place to reduce our suffering can so easily lead to an increase in our suffering has led Buddhists to refer to them as 'false refuges'. They seem as though they will offer safety and comfort but, if we over-use them, they instead offer anxiety and discomfort.

As we work to reduce our defences, one problem we will face is that they can be very hard to spot. When you use repression, by its very nature, you don't know you're doing it. Even the milder defences can be hard to identify. But you might reasonably suspect that you are relying heavily on defences if:

you lie awake at night anxious and uneasy but not really sure exactly *what* you are anxious and uneasy about

you are very quick to blame others when something goes wrong (and especially if your default position is that you are 'surrounded by idiots') you always have to be right – and you hold your viewpoint extremely strongly

you always have to be *doing* something.

We live busy lives these days, so the fact that you have little time to relax is understandable and an entirely natural consequence of the modern tech-enabled world. However, many of us have reached the point where simply doing nothing has become completely impossible because when we try to relax, instead of entering a pleasant world of calm, we instead enter a landscape of low-level unease, anxiety and restlessness.

Just *being* has become problematic. So instead, we make sure that we are continually *doing*.

If this is the case for you, it suggests your busyness and distraction might no longer be simply a natural result of a tough work schedule, or the 24/7 nature of modern life. You may be using busyness and distraction as a defence.

From noting my clients' reactions when I ask them to do nothing, I suspect that busyness and distraction are among the modern world's most prevalent defences. Our inability to sit down and reflect for a moment without reaching for our phones would amaze – and I think appal – earlier generations.

So, as we work to reduce our defences, busyness and distraction will be a good place to start because:

virtually everyone uses it sometimes

it's relatively easy to spot when we're doing it

it's a comparatively mild defence, so it's a gentle place to begin our work.

YOUR KEY TACTIC: 'MEET YOUR EDGE AND SOFTEN'

We must be careful as we dismantle our defences. It's necessary work if we want to fully realize our potential, but it will surface the uncomfortable stuff we've hidden below the defences. It is work that should be done slowly and carefully; your attitude should be one of gentle, kind curiosity and lots and lots of patience. Trust your intuition. If you feel there are issues hiding behind your defences that will be too difficult for you to cope with alone, then seek professional help before going too deep.

What we will do here is simply focus on chipping away at the edges of our defences. We will work with the easiest stuff and, in doing so, gradually build up our resilience. Actually, 'edge' is a good word. Chögyam Trungpa Rinpoche, who you will remember was the co-founder of the monastery in Scotland where Bowie studied, said that in a sense the whole spiritual path amounted to one simple instruction: 'Meet your edge and soften.'

Usually when we meet our edge, we tighten, we contract, we close down. Chögyam Trungpa says we should learn to do the opposite. When we notice that we are tightening, we should loosen. When we notice ourselves tensing, we should soften.

Notice, by the way, what a gentle instruction this is. Sometimes when I am asked to train corporate groups, the CEO or head of HR will ask me to 'take them right out of their comfort zone'. Yet, whether I'm coaching individuals, training groups or working with you in the pages of this book, it is not my intention to *take* anyone out of their comfort zone. I do, however, want you to end up with a greatly expanded comfort zone, which will have come about because you *choose* to take a step outside it. And then another. And then another. Or, to put it another way, because every time you met your edge, you softened.

Exercise: Interrupting mindless busyness, part 1 – doing nothing

To repeat, there's nothing wrong with being busy these days. Most of us are busy. The danger to our personal growth comes when we are relentlessly busy and *unable* to stop.

How often during a normal day do you do nothing? Absolutely nothing? Most people who I train or coach answer that question by saying 'never'. And many people consider the question itself slightly ridiculous. *What a waste of time! Why would I ever want to do nothing?* Because it's possible that your constant busyness is a defence; and if it is, then it is stopping you from feeling truly alive.

So, if you prefer, you could consider that in this exercise I am not asking you to do nothing. I am simply asking you to feel what it's like to be alive. And to notice how strongly you resist the idea that – instead of doing – you might simply *be*.

Anyway, I'd like you to sit and do nothing for fifteen minutes.

I'm not asking you to meditate here. Don't focus on your breath during this exercise, just do nothing. You will need to have a clock in view but don't stare at it. (And do not use your phone to check the time. Your phone should be in a different room.)

You're going to do nothing for fifteen minutes – or for as much of that fifteen minutes as you can stand. If during the fifteen minutes you reach the point where you decide you absolutely *can't* do any more, I want you to note that you have the feeling that you need to stop and then I want you to continue for another two minutes. *Then* stop. During those extra two minutes, examine the thoughts and feelings that arise.

OK, do that. Then continue reading.

If you lasted the whole fifteen minutes, well done. Research indicates that many people struggle to do nothing for more than about six minutes. Many of my clients manage considerably less.

If you stopped before the fifteen minutes, but you managed to stay for that additional two minutes, well done. You just met your edge, and you stayed there.

If you lasted the full fifteen minutes, reflect on what you thought and felt during that time and how often you felt the desire to get up and do something.

If you stopped before the fifteen minutes, focus particularly on the extra two minutes. When it became difficult to continue doing nothing, *why* was it difficult? What did you feel? What did you think? And what, if any, were your 'I should be…' thoughts?

Exercise: Interrupting mindless busyness, part 2 – doing one thing at a time

If you've ever done any mindfulness training, you will almost certainly have been given a raisin to eat. The exercise involves you eating the raisin very, very slowly indeed – noticing everything about the raisin, savouring all the sensations.

The learning from the exercise is that we usually eat mindlessly. By being mindful of the process, eating becomes much more enjoyable. We truly taste the food. It is genuinely astonishing how much flavour there is in one raisin. If you spend your life mindlessly shovelling snacks into your mouth while doing something else, you may never realize this.

Mindful eating also illustrates the general benefits of mindfulness over mindlessness.

Now we're going to do some mindful eating, but for a different reason. All of the above still applies. But through this exercise, I primarily want you to be aware of your desire to do other things, your search for distraction, your desire for busyness.

The exercise is simply this: I want you to prepare and eat a meal on your own without doing anything else at the same time. It doesn't matter which mealtime it is or what food you prepare. If you can't cook, you could simply make yourself a sandwich, but the exercise will tend to be more effective if preparing the food takes a while.

If you live with others, explain what you are doing and ask for some time alone in the kitchen.

Leave your phone and your laptop in another room. Switch off any TVs or radios or music players. Close any books, papers or magazines and ideally move them out of sight.

Then simply make your meal and eat it.

Try – gently – to keep your mind focused on the task at hand, and to eat the meal mindfully. As thoughts arise, let them go (as you have been doing in your meditation) and return to focus on the actual experience of eating. The food will taste better.

Mainly I want you to note when and how the urge to do something else arrives. When it happens, label it:

> I'm having the thought that I would like to look at my emails.
>
> I'm having the thought that I'm missing a programme on TV.
>
> I'm having a strong urge to just glance at that magazine and read the cover.
>
> I'm having the thought that this is stupid and I should just get my phone.

When you label the urge in this way, it should lose some of its power.

If the anxiety and restlessness and desire to do something builds up too much, shut your eyes, scan through the body to locate where you have tightened up, and – as Chögyam Trungpa said – just soften.

Take a slow deep breath and – as you breathe out slowly and deeply – let go of the tightness.

If the urge to do something builds up again, pause, and ask the urge:

> Why are you here?
>
> What is your purpose?
>
> What are you protecting me from?

Close your eyes and stay with this question for a moment. Then soften again. Breathe and soften.

Exercise: Awareness of your personas

As we've said, our persona is not necessarily a defence. It can be a perfectly healthy way of functioning.

However, just as busyness has become a prevalent defence in the modern world, I believe the advent of social media has accelerated the speed with which personas can mutate into unhealthy defences. Because the personas or masks we show the world have become more important to us, we invest more time in creating them, and we are more likely to have several of them existing in parallel.

This exercise is not designed to remove your persona. Instead, it is designed to help you be more aware of your persona, which will keep your persona as a healthy part of normal functioning and prevent it from becoming an unhealthy defence.

Thinking of all the 'masks' you wear in your life, fill in the following table.

	Partner	Children	Parents	Work	Boss	Social media 1	Social media 2
What do you dial up?							
What do you dial down?							
What do you invent?							
Can you just be yourself?							
If no, how much of the real you do you show?							
How do you feel about this?							
Could you bring more of the real you?							

Redraw this table on a large piece of paper, giving yourself plenty of room for your comments (neatness isn't important). Customize the top line to fit your life. If you don't have children, you don't need a 'Children' column; however, if your parents are dead, I would suggest filling in the parent column anyway, based on how you used to behave when you were with them. 'Social Media 1', 'Social Media 2', and so on will be Facebook, Twitter, LinkedIn, etc. depending on which platforms you use.

We'll walk through the table, using the 'Partner' column as an example. Go through the same process for each column.

What do you dial up? Which aspects of your personality do you favour when you are with your partner?

What do you dial down? Which aspects of your personality do you keep hidden or minimize when you're with your partner?

What do you invent? To what extent do you try to be somebody that you simply aren't because you think this will make your partner like you more?

Can you just be yourself? To what extent, when you're with your partner, can you completely let your guard down and simply be who you are? Could you tell them anything about yourself at all, without fear that they would judge or dislike you as a result?

If no, how much of the real you do you show? We're going to try to put a number on it here. In time spent with your partner, how much of the real you is evident, and how much of the real you is hidden? Score this out of ten, where ten would be 'my partner sees and knows absolutely everything about me,' and zero would be 'I keep all aspects of my real personality hidden.'

How do you feel about this? What does your score out of ten say about your relationship and how does this make you feel?

Could you bring more of the real you? Can you think of any ways in which you could be more you in this relationship? What specific steps could you take to achieve this?

Exercise: When am I most myself?

For a week, take a moment at the end of each day to review your day, and answer the question: 'When did I feel most myself today?'

Note the answers down.

Exercise: My self

Looking back over the answers to the previous exercises, but also thinking more widely about your life, answer the following questions:

Who lets me be myself?

In what places do I feel most myself?

At what times do I feel most myself?

During which activities, or in which situations, do I feel most myself?

Now finish this phrase:

When I am most myself, I am…

Finish this in any way you like: as a complete sentence; as a list of words; as a thousand-word essay; as a picture; as a diagram.

Your path: Going forward

After you've been through the exercises above, try the following.

1. Continue to meditate for at least three minutes a day. Longer would be great. But importantly, meditate long enough to notice your thoughts, to label them and let them go. Also notice and label any judgements.
2. Eat mindfully regularly. On a daily basis would be great, but at least once a week. If it's logistically impossible for you to eat a meal in this way because you're always with other people, then have a cup of tea or coffee mindfully. Do exactly the same, only focusing on the beverage and not allowing yourself to drift off into any secondary activity. Notice and mentally label any urge to do something else. You've heard of the Japanese tea ceremony. Now you have the 'My bedroom tea ceremony' or 'My kitchen tea ceremony' or, for that matter, even the 'Motorway services tea ceremony'.
3. Think about our initial question: Who are you?

   Your answers to the exercise will have helped you answer this question more fully. Hold on to this knowledge. Think about the tweaks that you can apply to your life to be a little bit more yourself, and start to apply them.

4. Do nothing regularly. Carve out a few minutes every day to do nothing. While you're doing this, practise:

    labelling your thoughts, feelings and urges to do something

    having a conversation with your thoughts and feelings ('Why are you here? Are you important? What are you trying to protect me from?')

    meeting your edge and softening. When the urge to get up and do something hits you, breathe, soften and remain.

5. Ask yourself this question: 'Who would I be without my defences?' As a thought experiment, live with that question for a week.

CHAPTER 4: ADDICTIONS

The life lesson: Remove yourself from the centre of the universe

Because I'm a drunk.

(Bowie, explaining to journalist Adrian Deevoy why he was drinking herbal tea at a party, 2003)

We came to believe that a power greater than ourselves could restore us to sanity.

(Step Two, Alcoholics Anonymous Twelve-Step Program)

I opened myself to the gentle indifference of the world. Finding it so much like myself – so like a brother, really – I felt that I had been happy and that I was happy again.

(Albert Camus, The Stranger*)*

BOWIE'S PATH

Unlike many other rock stars, Bowie's drug addiction was not an adjunct to a party lifestyle. Rather he used drugs to fuel his workaholism. He didn't get high, he got to work. When he finally began to clean up, he harnessed what he termed 'the powers of life itself'. His secret? Acceptance.

In July 1991, Carolyn Cowan, a make-up artist with a stellar career in the music industry (her clients had included Freddie Mercury, Bryan Ferry and Duran Duran), headed to Dublin to work on a video shoot for David Bowie.

A firm adherent of the rock-and-roll lifestyle, Cowan stayed up drinking till 3 a.m. the night before, then turned up for work at 5 a.m. She was expecting the video shoot to be a continuation of the fun, party lifestyle she had got used to, but when Bowie arrived on set what she actually got was an intervention.

'Bowie took one look at me – hungover, red-eyed and incoherent – and told me I was in trouble,' Cowan later recalled in a Mail Online article. 'He was in recovery from drug addiction and badly wanted me to get well too.'

Cowan resisted but, after three days of constant pressure, finally relented and accompanied Bowie to an Alcoholics Anonymous meeting. 'Everything he'd said had finally got through to me and I was so grateful,' she recalled.

Cowan had met Bowie at exactly the right time. Bowie had only recently committed to cleaning up, after decades of switching between addictions, or – at his worst – piling them up on top of each other. He had begun with cigarettes, initially stealing his father's. They would be Senior Service or – if John Jones was earning a bit more – Weights. Like many young men, Bowie began smoking because he perceived the habit as 'grown-up'. As a gawky, awkward youth, he was searching for attitude.

He held on to this idea that cigarettes convey a certain attitude throughout the 1970s. On the cover of his *Young Americans* album, he is holding a cigarette. The smoke curls up the whole left side of the cover, carefully stylized by the art director into what would at the time have been seen as a symbol of elegant sophistication.

A year later, touring in his Thin White Duke persona, Bowie would tuck a packet of Gitanes into his pocket, making sure that it remained visible – a flash of Gallic blue to catch the eye amid the Duke's relentlessly monochrome attire. He had latched on to Gitanes for typically Bowie reasons: aesthetics, not taste. He first discovered the brand while working as an illustrator at an ad agency in the mid-1960s, and it was the pack's design that appealed.

The visual element also ruled on stage; he would always light cigarettes with matches because he felt it was more theatrical. His cigarette was a prop. It was also, like so much else in his life, a defence – a way of avoiding emotional connection – as he told Jarvis Cocker in a 1997 conversation in *The Big Issue*: 'The cigarette became symbolic of a certain kind of removed identity… that I don't *have* to be singing these songs, I'm just doing you a favour.'

As well as a prop and a defence, his cigarette was also a genuine addiction. He admitted to Cocker that the ritual and theatre element was long gone by the time of their conversation; the elegant matches had been replaced by a mundane Bic lighter, the cultish Gitanes by mainstream Marlboros, and smoking was 'just another bloody thing that I do'.

During the mid-1970s rush of fame, he supplemented cigarettes with cocaine but, where other rock stars might have used the drug to fuel a glamorous party lifestyle, Bowie used it simply to fuel another of his addictions: his workaholism. His wealth and success gave him access to large quantities of pharmaceutical-grade Merck cocaine – the same pure quality that had been used by Freud in experimental treatments in the 1890s, and the stuff of dreams for most addicts. But when in 2000, the *NME* named Bowie the most influential artist of all time and talked to him about his career, he stressed the purely functional role that drugs had played in his life: 'I didn't really use them for hedonistic purposes. I didn't really go out very much. I wasn't getting totally out of it and going to clubs and all that. I was really just working. I would work days in a row without sleep. It wasn't a joyful, euphoric kind of thing. I was driving myself to a point of insanity.'

This is not an exaggeration. By 1976, as we'll see in more detail in Chapter 6, he had hit the 'rock bottom' of addiction legend. Although he began to tackle his cocaine habit in 1976, he initially simply switched his addictive behaviour to alcohol. It wasn't until 1989 that he entered Alcoholics Anonymous – signalling his increased commitment to finally ending his addictions. What did he learn from AA that helped him grapple with his addictions? To answer that, we need to study the back of his left leg.

A FROG, A DOLPHIN... AND GOD

In 1991, on one of his regular trips to Japan, Bowie got an intriguing tattoo inked on the back of his left calf. It showed a man riding a dolphin while holding a frog in the palm of his left hand, alongside some text in Japanese Katakana. Bowie, who drew the original of the artwork himself, never fully explained the significance of the frog or the dolphin. But he did reveal that the Japanese inscription was a translation of the Serenity Prayer.

Reinhold Niebuhr is generally considered to be the most important US theologian of the twentieth century. He was a great influence on Dr Martin Luther King, who praised him as a man with 'great prophetic vision', and was also one of Barack Obama's favourite thinkers. But he's best known for writing this:

> God, grant me the serenity to accept
> the things I cannot change,
>
> The courage to change the things I can,
>
> And the wisdom to know the difference.

This simple prayer has been widely adopted by Alcoholics Anonymous and other twelve-step programs (often in a pluralized form with the 'I' becoming 'we'). On the rare occasions when Bowie discussed – or at least alluded to – Alcoholics Anonymous, he suggested it was the Serenity Prayer's idea of acceptance that was crucial to him in his recovery. He stated clearly that it kept him on the course, that it spoke to 'my knowledge of the powers of life itself', and referred to a particular passage in an Alcoholics Anonymous handbook that resonates closely with the Serenity Prayer:

> Acceptance is the answer to *all* my problems today. When I am disturbed, it is because I find some person, place, thing or situation – some fact of my life – unacceptable to me. I can find no serenity until I accept that person, place, thing or situation as being exactly the way it is supposed to be at this moment. Nothing, absolutely nothing, happens in God's world by mistake. Until I could accept my alcoholism, I could not stay sober; unless I accept life completely on life's terms, I cannot be happy.

As soon as we start referencing Alcoholics Anonymous, we inevitably encounter God. As Bowie embraced the Twelve-Step Program, did he also fully embrace God? Perhaps briefly, during the early 1990s, but then he quickly reverted to his 'almost an atheist' default, constantly questioning, struggling with and trying to make sense of his spiritual side.

In fact, when he entered a twelve-step program in 1989, Bowie was not so much meeting God as being reunited with ideas that had been vitally important to him twenty years earlier because – as we'll see in the next section – the Twelve-Step approach is heavily based on the ideas of Carl Jung, and the idea of acceptance that was so important to Bowie was an echo from his early Buddhist studies.

THE LIFE LESSON: REMOVE YOURSELF FROM THE CENTRE OF THE UNIVERSE

Addicts are asked to open themselves up to a higher power. Where does this idea come from? And how and why does it help addicts to heal? As we investigate these questions, we will discover that you don't have to be an addict to benefit from letting go of control and pursuing an attitude of acceptance.

Just before I began to write this chapter, I was listening to a science programme on the radio. The subject was 'the chemistry of love' and, after much talk of dopamine, oxytocin and endorphins, the show concluded with the comment that 'love activates the addiction centres of the brain'. *Surely* that's the wrong way round? Surely what's actually going on is that addiction activates the love centres of the brain?

There is consensus that addiction is caused by three factors, but little consensus over which is the most important. These factors are:

> *Genetic*: the belief that some people are genetically more predisposed to addiction than others
>
> *Developmental*: the belief that what is happening around the person at the time they begin the addiction is crucial

Behavioural: the belief that people who have adverse childhood experiences are more likely to become addicts.

In this chapter we are going to focus exclusively on the behavioural side of things because we want to examine addiction specifically as a strategy to avoid distress. When we look at addiction through a behavioural lens, what we are seeing is a person who reacts to their distress without first stopping to observe it and reacts in an unhealthy way. An addict who is recovering or healing is a person who has managed to start observing their distress and therefore, instead of reacting to it unthinkingly and unhealthily, is able to respond to it in a healthier way.

We all sometimes react to distress without observing it first, and often in unhealthy ways. If we can learn to observe our distress first, and make healthier choices, then we have moved an important step forward on our journey. That's why an examination of the principles that help some addicts to heal can provide valuable lessons for all of us. So, in the context of this book, when we ask 'what causes addiction?' we are asking a very specific question.

'What causes addiction?' can mean (at least) three different things:

1. Why is one person more likely to become chemically dependent on a substance than another person?
2. What are the factors that cause a person to choose a specific addictive substance or behaviour?

3. What is the root factor that creates the basic need/anxiety/restlessness/discomfort within a person that they wish to avoid, that makes them want to engage in the behaviour that subsequently becomes addictive?

A LOVE-SHAPED HOLE

For our purposes, the third of these questions is the important one. And we'll find the very essence of the answer in a heartbreaking quote from Dr Gabor Maté's fascinating book on addiction, *In the Realm of the Hungry Ghosts*. The book draws heavily on his work at a Vancouver residence and resource centre for the homeless and at harm-reduction and safe-injection facilities. Maté quotes a twenty-seven-year-old sex worker:

> 'The first time I did heroin,' she said to me, 'it felt like a warm soft hug.' In that phrase she told her life story and summed up the psychological and chemical cravings of all substance-dependent addicts.

To return to the phraseology of the radio show: the heroin activated the love centres of her brain. Perhaps it helped to fill a void left by an absence of love in her life. Or perhaps – as we're about to discover – it helped repair an emotional deprivation suffered by her mother or a trauma suffered by her grandfather.

Maté's work also draws on his own addictive behaviour, which he relates back to his traumatic infancy. Maté was born in Budapest two months before the Nazis invaded the country. In another of his books, *Scattered Minds*, he tells of the time, a few days after the Nazis arrived in Budapest itself, when his mother called the doctor, asking him to come and see young Gabor because the baby had been crying non-stop for two days.

> 'I'll come, of course,' the doctor replied, 'but I should tell you: *all* my Jewish babies are crying.' Now, what did Jewish infants know of Nazis, World War II, racism, genocide? What they knew – or rather absorbed – was their parents' anxiety. They inhaled fear, ingested sorrow. Yet were they not loved? No less than children anywhere.

I hope it's evident that no blame can be attached to Dr Maté's mother for his later-life addictive behaviour as he sought to self-soothe. No parent could shield a baby from the fear and anxiety caused by such horrors. Equally we can't blame Dr Maté if this potentially addiction-prompting need for comfort has been passed on to the next generation.

Why might comfort-seeking or addiction-prompting behaviours be passed on? Fascinating studies with rats show that rat pups who receive specific mothering behaviour (licking and grooming) have high oxytocin receptor expressions in key brain regions. This means that in later life they will be more resilient and handle stress well. If mothers are prevented from performing – or are unable to perform – this licking and grooming, their pups will not handle stress well. Crucially these less resilient rats pass their lack of resilience on to the next generation.

If we are the same (and we are genetically, biologically and behaviourally very similar to rats), we can see that an individual might have a loving and supportive childhood and yet still carry into later life a need for self-soothing that they might assuage with addictive behaviour; the root cause might lie one or two (or more) generations in the past.

Dr Maté's experience is, of course, extreme. But how many of us have grandparents who were traumatized or separated by war, or great-grandparents who fled persecution across boundaries, or older ancestors whose lives we simply know nothing about who may have suffered all sorts of traumas? And how many of us therefore go through life with a love-shaped hole inside of us? Or should that be a god-shaped hole?

A GOD-SHAPED HOLE

Rowland Hazard III was a successful American businessman in the first half of the last century. He held board positions on several companies across several different industries including chemicals, banking and manufacturing, and also played an active role in local politics. But his claim to fame is that he was an alcoholic.

More than that, he was one of the most important alcoholics in history.

Hazard heard of Jung's ideas and was fascinated by them. He sought out the pioneering psychologist in 1931 and became his patient, staying in his care for several months, after which he stopped drinking. Later in the year, while on a trip to Africa, he relapsed and was taken by friends back to Switzerland to see Jung again.

Jung told Hazard that there was nothing more psychoanalysis could do for him, and that his case was hopeless.

That sounds like the end of the story but, in fact, it's the beginning. As Bill Wilson, the co-founder of Alcoholics Anonymous, wrote in a letter to Jung in 1961: 'this candid and humble statement of yours was beyond doubt, the first foundation stone upon which our society has been built'.

The second foundation stone was what Jung said next. He told Hazard that his only hope for recovery would be a vital spiritual experience, adding that Hazard would be unlikely to find one of these in a church (a comment perhaps heavily coloured by the fact that Jung's father was a pastor who lost his faith but continued in his role anyway). In his reply to Wilson, Jung wrote of Hazard: 'His craving for alcohol was the equivalent, on a low level, of the spiritual thirst of our being for wholeness, expressed in medieval language: the union with God.'

These ideas were much in Jung's mind in the early 1930s, as shown in this passage from his 1933 book, *Modern Man in Search of a Soul*:

> I have treated many hundreds of patients. Among those in the second half of life – that is to say, over 35 – there has not been one whose problem in the last resort was not that of finding a religious outlook on life. It is safe to say that every one of them fell ill because he had lost that which the living religions of every age have given their followers, and

none of them has really been healed who did not regain his religious outlook.

Jung's opinion that a spiritual experience was necessary was not given lightly. In his correspondence with Wilson (which took place thirty years later), Jung revealed that, at the time he was treating Hazard, he had to be extremely careful how he talked about spirituality or God because his techniques were radical and, in order for them to be accepted, he needed people to see them as scientific. As someone who was bringing new ideas to the public, he wrote, he was used to being 'misunderstood in every possible way'. Note that he referred to the idea of a 'union with God' as 'medieval language' – Jung admitted that he struggled to express his ideas in language that would be truly understood in the contemporary world.

Wilson, however, had completely understood his meaning: 'Your words really carried authority, because you seemed to be neither wholly a theologian nor a pure scientist. Therefore, you seemed to stand with us in that no-man's land that lies between the two… You spoke a language of the heart that we could understand.'

Jung said that to achieve such wholeness – to regain your religious outlook – you had to walk on a path that would lead to higher understanding.

In search of his own spiritual experience, in the mid-1930s Rowland Hazard joined the Oxford Group, an evangelical Christian movement dedicated to pursuing personal change. Here he met an alcoholic called Ebby Thatcher, whom he helped to stop drinking. Thatcher then took a combination of Hazard's

Jung-inspired beliefs and Oxford Group principles to his friend and former drinking buddy Bill Wilson. Wilson was reportedly aghast at the idea that his old friend Ebby had 'got religion', but he soon underwent his own spiritual experience and stopped drinking, and in 1935 he co-founded Alcoholics Anonymous.

Decades later, in his reply to Wilson's 1961 letter, Jung summed up his message to Hazard: 'You see, "alcohol" in Latin is *spiritus*, and you use the same word for the highest religious experience as well as for the most depraving poison. The helpful formula therefore is: *spiritus contra spiritum*.' The AA handbook translates this key phrase as: 'Higher power overcomes alcoholism'.

We can see the influence of Jung filtered through Hazard and the Oxford movement quite clearly in the first two tenets of Alcoholics Anonymous:

1. We admitted we were powerless over alcohol – that our lives had become unmanageable.
2. Came to believe that a Power greater than ourselves could restore us to sanity.

THE GOD BARRIER

It's telling that even the man who went on to found Alcoholics Anonymous was apparently appalled initially at the idea that God might have something to do with his potential 'cure'. Note how the word 'God' isn't introduced in the second tenet. Instead it comes in the third and, as soon as it appears, it is immediately qualified:

> 3. Made a decision to turn our will and our lives over to the care of God as we understood Him.

How many people have considered attending an Alcoholics Anonymous meeting, or perhaps even got through the door and sat down, only to encounter the word 'God' and think, 'Well, this isn't for me'?

Can those who don't believe in God find helpful advice in a sentence that has the word 'God' in it, or is the word 'God' a barrier that some of us just can't get over? There are valuable learnings for *everyone* in the first three tenets of AA, and if the God word stops you from considering them, that's a problem (for you, not God).

We don't have to believe in God to get the benefit of these ideas (that's made clear in the 'as we understood Him' qualification). Crucially, it doesn't matter what we call the Higher Power – or even what we think it is – but what really *does* matter is how we see ourselves in relation to it or, to rephrase that, what we think the Higher Power is there for.

In my career as a music journalist I once interviewed a famous singer who hadn't had a hit for many years. During the interview she explained that she was a Buddhist. I was intrigued and asked how that showed itself in her life. 'I chant,' she declared, and then proceeded to explain that she had needed £50,000 to make her new album, so she had chanted for it every day for several weeks, and eventually the money 'turned up'. Pressed to explain how exactly £50,000 had 'turned up', the singer reluctantly admitted that her manager had been negotiating a deal with a record company throughout the period she was chanting – but she was adamant it was the chanting that had tipped the scales in her favour.

Buddhists may chant as a way of memorizing and repeating teachings (this would for centuries have been the main way of preserving the teachings), or they may use mantras to focus attention. In different forms of Buddhism, chanting will perform different functions. But they don't chant to get money. However, it's not hard to see where this singer got the idea that you chant or pray or talk to God in order to get stuff; in our culture there is a child-friendly version of prayer where we simply ask God to give us things. Oddly, though, some of us never grow out of that childlike position. Some of us never notice the line in the Lord's Prayer that says 'thy will be done' – that the Higher Power is going to do whatever it wants. There are hints in the rest of the AA code that the Higher Power will somehow look after us, but it will look after us *on its own terms*. Not on ours. This is the crucial point. The Higher Power is not there to give us what we want.

This is summed up beautifully in the old Jewish saying: 'God is not nice. God is not your uncle. God is an earthquake.'

Here, in this understanding of what the Higher Power *isn't*, is where AA meets Buddhism. And then, really quite surprisingly, they both meet the decidedly atheist philosophies of the mid-twentieth century: existentialism and absurdism. They meet in the understanding that God/the Higher Power/nature/the universe/the Tao – call it what you want – is not here to give you what you want.

To put that another way: the universe does not revolve around you. Why should it?

ACCEPTANCE

This, at heart, is what acceptance really means: the world is as it is. The world is not supposed to be the way you want it. Acceptance is, effectively, the opposite of the Buddhist concept of attachment, which you'll remember is said to be the cause of all suffering. Attachment, as we discovered in Chapter 2, is a tricky idea to articulate clearly. But 'expecting the world to be (or to become) exactly the way you want it' comes close. Our suffering arises because God/the Higher Power/nature/the universe/the Tao refuses to go along with our wishes.

If attachment is the cause of suffering, then acceptance must be… well, let's return to the AA quote that meant so much to Bowie: 'Acceptance is the answer to *all* my problems today. When I am disturbed, it is because I find some person, place, thing or situation – some fact of my life – unacceptable to me. I can find no serenity until I accept that person, place, thing or situation as being exactly the way it is supposed to be at this moment.'

Acceptance arises when we let go of our desire to have everything turn out our way, when we allow things to be as they are, when we remove ourselves from the centre of the universe. But how hard it is for us to accept that the world is as it should be, when it isn't how *we* want it to be! Why is this such a struggle? Why, in short, are we so attached to attachment?

Our desire to have everything the way we want it is undoubtedly made stronger by many factors in our modern culture:

- advertising that promises the next product or service will make your life better
- technology that removes even the tiniest delay and gratifies our desires
- capitalism that rewards companies and the people who run them every time they succeed in developing an innovation that meets our needs – especially when they are simultaneously *creating* the need they are meeting because we didn't know it existed before the product did.

I remember years ago a stand-up comedian doing a hilarious routine when electric windows were first introduced in some high-end cars. 'What exactly is the problem,' the comedian asked, 'to which this is the solution?' They then mimed winding down the window manually, while groaning and grunting with pretend effort, finally collapsing in utter exhaustion. The crowd roared: imagine the idiot car manufacturers thinking that we couldn't even wind down a window! And yet now, the very idea that you couldn't open the car window at the touch of a button would seem like an appalling deprivation. Capitalism has successfully created yet another 'need'.

Modern culture may have made things worse but it's not the root cause of the difficulty we experience in letting go of our desire to have everything our way.

Perhaps we find it so hard to remove ourselves from the centre of the universe because we so vividly are at the centre of *our* universe. Because the world comes to us via our sense perceptions, we are literally in the middle of it. How confusing, then, to be told that the universe doesn't revolve around us at all – however wise the people who may tell us, and however often down the ages this message is repeated.

It isn't just the Buddha, Jung and the AA who have suggested that our path to sanity and happiness lies in letting go of the idea that we are the centre of the universe, that everything should revolve around us and that we should get everything we want. It's present in pretty much all the world's wisdom traditions. It's the very heart of Taoism: we should learn to flow with the universe, not waste our effort trying to get the universe to follow our desires.

We also resist the idea because it seems so paradoxical and counterintuitive that, once you remove yourself from the centre of the universe, things can start to get better. As that passage in the AA handbook that Bowie liked to reference put it: 'Until I could accept my alcoholism, I could not stay sober; unless I accept life completely on life's terms, I cannot be happy.'

There are two exquisitely paradoxical ideas right there:

1. I can't change till I accept how I am.
2. I won't get what I want till I stop trying to get what I want.

While we are talking about things that are paradoxical and counterintuitive, this would be a perfect moment to bring in the French philosopher and novelist Albert Camus, whose novel *The Stranger* was one of Bowie's favourites. Camus is closely associated with absurdist philosophy. Absurdism regards the universe as essentially meaningless, and argues that since the world is meaningless, so are our lives; but then adds that, once you accept there is no meaning in the universe, you can find some meaning in this meaninglessness.

Even in this paradoxical and Godless universe, the secret of happiness turns out to be exactly the same as it is in a God-driven one.

In *The Stranger*, the protagonist Meursault kills a man and is sentenced to death. He is considered to be a soulless monster not just because of the murder he has committed but also because he did not cry at his mother's funeral. Meursault says he has simply never had any feelings at all about any of his actions. As his execution draws near, he's visited by a priest. Initially, he rages at the priest and at the meaninglessness of the world, but then suddenly his attitude changes. In this most extreme of circumstances he finds acceptance: 'I opened myself to the gentle indifference of the world. Finding it so much like myself – so like a brother, really – I felt that I had been happy and that I was happy again.'

Opening yourself to the gentle indifference of the world is surely the same thing as turning your will over to a Higher Power – as long as we understand that the Higher Power is not there to give us everything we want.

From evangelical Christians to atheist existentialists, from Buddhists to Jungians, the message is the same: acceptance.

YOUR PATH

Now we'll look at ways to reduce the power of cravings and addictions. We'll also explore some techniques to encourage the attitude of acceptance that so many wisdom traditions agree is fundamentally important.

Before we start let's be clear on what acceptance *doesn't* mean.

It doesn't mean you have to put up with abuse or bullying or violence. It doesn't mean you can't act to change anything ever. It doesn't mean you're not allowed to want anything ever again.

It means that – on a spectrum from wanting absolutely everything to go our way to allowing everything to be exactly as it is – most of us are slightly too far towards the former and would benefit from moving slightly further towards the latter. With that in mind, the exercises in this section have three objectives:

1. to reduce the power of your cravings
2. to increase your ability to reach a state of acceptance
3. to nudge your perception of the world slightly so that you find it easier to realize that you are not the centre of the universe.

That last objective assumes that you currently think you are the centre of the universe, but I am not implying you are particularly arrogant or self-centred; if you're reading this book, you're almost certainly quite the opposite. It's just that we all have the natural human thought that we would like to get what we want. And this thought, as we have already discussed, is not necessarily helpful. Shortly, we will look at a meditation specifically designed to reduce craving and help you tackle addictions. But, before we do that, I want to modify our regular meditation practice by adding a new visualization.

Exercise: Letting thoughts go – the bubble and feather visualization

Hopefully up till now you've been meditating every day for at least three minutes – ideally longer – simply focusing on your breath and letting thoughts go. Next time you do this, I would like you to add a new element.

As before, find a reasonably quiet, reasonably private place.

Sit in a state of relaxed alertness, comfortable but not too comfortable so that you don't fall asleep. Close your eyes. Take a few slow deep breaths and gradually tune in to the rhythm of the in breath and the out breath.

Maintain your focus on your breath. As in previous meditations, notice when thoughts occur, label them and let them go. Then return to your breath.

This time, however, when you have a thought, notice it and label it as a thought. But then visualize the thought as a bubble floating across your mind – as if a child is blowing bubbles nearby.

As you let the thought go, visualize touching the bubble lightly with a feather. The bubble bursts and the thought is gone. Return to your breath. Continue focusing on the breath, and use the same visualization technique every time a thought occurs.

After a few minutes, gently bring the meditation to an end by slowly opening your eyes.

The purpose of this visualization is to emphasize two things:

1. *Thoughts are in fact very slight things.* They do not necessarily have the weight and importance that we often ascribe to them.
2. *Letting go of thoughts is a gentle process.* We are not pushing them away. We're not repressing them. We are not considering them bad. We're not considering ourselves bad for having them. We're just ever so gently letting them go.

Exercise: Meditation for reducing craving

This is a meditation to employ when you feel the cravings that will normally lead you to pursue your addictive behaviour. It will not always be appropriate; you can't do this in public. Although, when you have done this meditation several times, you will find you can employ the same techniques from the meditation without sitting down and shutting your eyes, no matter where the craving strikes. To begin with, however, its main use will be when you are hit by cravings at home.

As with other meditations, sit somewhere peaceful and reasonably quiet (absolute silence is not necessary). Sit in a state of relaxed alertness, close your eyes and take a few long, slow deep breaths.

As much as possible, given that you are being assailed by your craving, try to focus on your breath.

Tune in to the in breath and the out breath. Align yourself with the rhythm that flows through your body. If you find this harder to do than usual, don't beat yourself up about this. Accept the reality of the situation. You're not trying to reach an ideal meditative state; you want to work *with* your reality, not against it.

As with our other meditations, simply notice whatever interrupts your focus on the breath. It's likely to be associated with your craving (but might not be).

If it's a thought, label it as a thought. If it is a physical sensation, label it as a physical sensation. If it is a visual image of the object of your addiction, label it as a visual image. Say to yourself: 'This is a thought.' Or: 'This is a physical sensation.' Or: 'This is a visual image.'

Then let the thought or sensation or image go. If you're able to use the bubble and feather visualization, please do as this will be very helpful.

Return the focus to the breath. When your focus is interrupted again, repeat the procedure.

Experiment with labelling in a slightly different way: 'I am observing a thought.' Or: 'I am observing a physical sensation.' Or: 'I am observing a visual image.'

Once again, use the bubble and feather visualization as you let the thought, sensation or image go.

Continue the process for several minutes. Notice if the frequency or intensity of thoughts, images or sensations changes, and remember to return the focus to the breath.

Then, in your own time, bring the meditation to a close.

The purpose of the meditation is that you observe your craving before reacting to it. As you meditate to observe craving, there are several benefits:

- You are activating your parasympathetic nervous system, which is calming you down and reducing stress. As stress increases cravings, by reducing stress you may be able to also reduce the power of your craving.
- You are occupying the part of your mind that develops cravings. The Elaborated Intrusion Theory of Desire suggests that cravings build quickly from an initial intrusive thought to become overwhelming as the initial thought is elaborated. By meditating, you may be able to short-circuit this build-up.
- The Elaborated Intrusion Theory of Desire also suggests that the thoughts, sensations and images that accompany craving are heavily emotionally charged.

By observing them in a neutral way you are reducing or removing the emotional charge.

- The theory also states that negative emotions induce a sense of generalized deprivation that we then attribute to being deprived of the object of our craving. By stopping and observing, we separate any general sense of deprivation from the target of our addiction or craving.
- In terms of mild cravings, a meditation like this can reduce or even stop the craving. In terms of more serious addictions, it is a helpful tool to start to give you some sense of control over what is occurring.

Exercise: Notice your moments of not accepting

During the normal course of the day, get into the habit of actively noticing when you feel you do not want to accept the current situation. This won't be hard to do. You will have a clear emotional clue. You will be angry, sad or frustrated. When you notice that you have such a feeling, try to also notice the lack of acceptance that lies behind it. Again, labelling will be helpful. 'This is a moment of non-acceptance' or 'This is a moment when I do not want to accept the world as it is.'

Now employ the distinction highlighted in the Serenity Prayer. Is this something you can change? If so, put a plan in place to do so. If not, continue with this exercise.

Once you have noticed and labelled the non-acceptance, move to compassion. Remind yourself that millions of other people struggle with the same issues. They too do not want to accept the things that you do not want to accept. Say to yourself: 'I am not alone in this. Many other people feel the same.' Allow yourself to feel compassion for the other people going through what you're going through now. Stay with that feeling of compassion. Allow it to grow and develop.

And then include *yourself* in that feeling of compassion.

Exercise: Where have I tightened?

You will remember that Chögyam Trungpa Rinpoche advised us to 'meet your edge and soften'. When we have a moment of non-acceptance, when we have a craving, when we resort to our addictive behaviour, we are meeting our edge and tightening.

Sometimes we will not be able to deal with this in a skilful way. When we are overwhelmed, we may give in to our addiction or other unhelpful behaviour. It can be helpful to review this behaviour at the end of the day, or perhaps the next day. Not to be critical of ourselves – life is tough and we're only human – but to give some kind attention to the distress that may have led us to this 'edge'.

Close your eyes. Take a few deep breaths and scan through your body. Ask yourself: 'Where have I tightened?'

Keep breathing slowly and deeply. Keep asking the question: 'Where have I tightened?' Your body will tell you. Focus on the area that has physically tightened. Breathe into the area. As you breathe in, reflect: 'What did I tighten against? Why did I tighten against it?' Offer yourself some compassion: 'This was a difficult moment for me.' As you breathe out, soften. Perhaps you weren't able to do this at the time, but you can do it now. With each out breath, just soften, letting go of the tightness and the stress.

Take as much time as you need. Then you may choose to scan again, asking, 'Where else have I tightened?' If you find more tightness in other areas of your body, repeat the process.

Exercise: Removing yourself from the centre of the universe

This is an exercise you can do every time you have a conversation with anyone you care about. (You can do it with strangers too.) When you're about to start a conversation, actively create an agenda that is not centred on you.

Do not come to the conversation with a list of all the things you want to say, all the demands you want to make, all the points you want to prove, all the complaints you want to moan about, all your irritations accumulated during the day so far. Instead, come with three intentions:

1. To begin the conversation with *them*
2. To find out what they are feeling
3. To ask twice as many questions as you make statements.

Beginning with them. Resist the temptation to begin the conversation by saying, 'I've had a terrible day,' or 'you'll never guess what happened to me,' or by launching into your story about your terrible commute or the appalling customer-service experience you've recently endured. Instead, begin by finding out about their day, their morning, their week, their current state of mind.

What are they feeling? You can just ask someone how they're feeling, of course, but in our modern culture the usual answer is 'fine'. Some people will welcome a further enquiry – 'How are you really feeling?' – and others won't. So this practice is not necessarily about asking questions; it is about simply observing. Make part of your agenda for the conversation to notice tone of voice, body language and what is left unsaid.

Twice as many questions. This is as simple as it sounds, but not easy to do. Make a commitment that during the conversation you will ask twice as many questions about the other person as you will make statements about yourself. This does not mean that you should arrive with a list of twenty questions or that you should interrogate them like a detective. Most can be follow-up questions: 'Why was that?' or: 'What happened then?' or: 'How did that make you feel?'

Your path: Going forward

After you've been through the exercises above, try the following.

1. Continue your meditation practice. Try to increase the amount of time you spend meditating each day – noticing thoughts, labelling them and letting them go. Include the bubble and feather visualization if you have found this helpful.

2. In the *Notice your moments of not accepting* and *Where have I tightened* exercises, you were asked to offer yourself compassion. What did that feel like? Did you feel any resistance to the idea of feeling compassionate towards yourself? Reflect on how easy or difficult you find it to be kind to yourself.

3. In this chapter we read that Bill Wilson wrote to Jung: 'You spoke a language of the heart that we could understand.' Reflect on what this means to you. As you go through your day, notice if you meet anyone who you feel speaks a language of the heart. Are you able to speak a language of the heart? Who have you known in your life who was able to do this?

4. Ask yourself the question: 'Who am I if I am not the centre of the universe?' As a thought experiment, stay with that question for a week. If you could more fully accept that the world does not revolve around you and that you shouldn't get everything the way you want it, how would that change your relationships with:

    Your partner?

    Your children?

    Your parents?

    Your friends?

    Your work colleagues?

    Strangers?

CHAPTER 5: THOUGHTS

The life lesson: Change your relationship with your thoughts

I think if [a person] is in isolation, instead of receiving the whole world as his home, he tends to create a micro-world inside himself. And it's that peculiar part of the human mind that fascinates me – the small universes that can be created inside the mind – some of them fairly schizophrenic and quite off the wall.

(Bowie, 1979)

Nothing can harm you as much as your own untamed thoughts.

(Buddha)

I have tried in my work to free myself from my own head.

(John Cage)

BOWIE'S PATH

Bowie famously employed 'cut-up' methods of writing, where songs are randomly constructed with no clear narrative flow. He did this to take his mind to places it would not normally go – to break away from routine thinking. He wanted to generate a childlike sense of play, free from self-criticism and judgement.

Why does an artist create?

David Bowie was very clear about why he wrote songs. He had a definite purpose in mind: to help him navigate the world by increasing self-knowledge. His writing was primarily a quest to discover something inside himself – but also something beyond himself.

In 1997 in the documentary film *Inspirations* he told director Michael Apted that, more than thirty years after he had begun his writing career, he found it valuable to hold on to this purpose. He urged himself:

> Always remember that the reason you initially started working was that there was something inside yourself that you felt that – if you could manifest it in some way – you

> would understand more about yourself and how you co-exist with the rest of society.

In this we hear echoes of the shy, alienated, young David Jones at the beginning of his career. We also hear that – even after a quarter of a century of success, fame and critical acclaim – he knows he is still a work in progress.

In another interview that same year, with Paul Ill in *The Music Paper*, Bowie stressed that this quest for self-understanding had always had a spiritual aspect:

> Everything I've written is about: Who is my God? How does He show Himself? What is my higher stage, my higher being?

Given the importance of this quest to Bowie, and given that he believed his work was his best vehicle for this self-discovery, the way he went about his work seems at first glance to be quite extraordinary.

If we think about how writers create, what do we imagine happening? Perhaps we think of a poet wandering in nature, communing with eternal forces before putting pen to paper. Perhaps we see a singer-songwriter, acoustic guitar in hand, eyes shut, face contorted with the effort of channelling their innermost feelings. Perhaps we think of a tortured artist like Van Gogh exorcizing his demons with dramatic brushstrokes and vibrant colours.

However we imagine this, we tend to think in terms of art as self-expression, as a way of getting something that is inside the artist out into the world. And this is what Bowie said: there was something inside him that he needed to manifest.

Yet, in trying to uncover this 'something', Bowie went out of his way to avoid straightforward self-expression. In examining himself, he deliberately chose to not listen to himself. In searching for meaning, he avoided meaning.

In trying to discover who he was, Bowie's key technique was to stop himself from thinking, or at least to stop himself from thinking the way he naturally thought. Throughout his career he borrowed or developed a series of techniques to disrupt his normal thinking process to block any attempt to make sense and to interrupt any logical or narrative flow in his work.

For someone looking for himself, he seemed extraordinarily uninterested in the products of his mind.

Bowie's method of uncovering the secrets within himself was to engage in a series of utterly random experiments. The first randomizing technique he employed to distance himself from his normal thinking was 'cut-ups'. He said he used cut-ups in roughly 40 per cent of his work. He certainly used the technique heavily during his 1970s heyday. He attributed his initial discovery of cut-ups to his reading of William Burroughs, who had developed the idea with Brion Gysin – both members of the Beat Generation that Terry had brought to Bowie's attention. Bowie was also heavily influenced in his use of randomizing techniques by John Cage, the composer who had revolutionized classical music in the 1950s with his compositions created through chance operations. To create his solo piano piece 'Music of Changes', for example, Cage had used the random-number-generating properties of the ancient Chinese divination text the *I Ching* to determine pitch, volume, tempo and note duration.

In fact, the idea of creating art through random processes goes back even further – to the Dadaist movement of the first two decades of the twentieth century. The Dada pioneer Tristan Tzara explained the process perfectly in a subsection of his work *Dada Manifesto on Feeble Love and Bitter Love* published in 1920 and called 'How to Make a Dadaist Poem':

> To make a Dadaist poem:
>
> - Take a newspaper.
> - Take a pair of scissors.
> - Choose an article as long as you are planning to make your poem.
> - Cut out the article.
> - Then cut out each of the words that make up this article and put them in a bag.
> - Shake it gently.
> - Then take out the scraps one after the other and place them in the order in which they left the bag.
> - Copy conscientiously.
> - The poem will be like you.

Burroughs and Gysin would often cut out phrases or whole sentences rather than just single words, but their method was essentially the same. Bowie can be seen employing the technique in the 1975 documentary *Cracked Actor*.

A century after Dada we are a little more used to such avant-garde ideas, but the part of the process that still stretches our credulity is the idea that 'the poem will be like you'. How can a technique that so ruthlessly removes the idea of self-expression tell us anything about the artist?

NEXT DOOR TO HELL

If the cut-ups technique seems unusual, Bowie's next ploy to move away from his normal modes of thinking was more than just surprising; given what we know of his history, it is positively shocking. In his quest for new ways of thinking, he headed straight towards the way of thinking that he most feared: schizophrenia.

On at least two occasions – once in the 1970s and once in the 1990s – Bowie and his regular collaborator Brian Eno visited Gugging.

The Maria Gugging Psychiatric Clinic is a psychiatric institution on the outskirts of Vienna. There, in the late 1950s, a psychiatrist called Leo Navratil embarked on a radical new form of treatment. He asked his patients to produce drawings. Originally this was purely for diagnostic purposes, but he quickly believed he had discovered genuine artistic talent – a verdict later confirmed by Jean Dubuffet, the French artist who had coined the term 'Art Brut'.

Since 1970 the work of patients at the clinic – usually referred to as 'the Gugging Artists' – has been presented in galleries and museums, and they are considered among the world's foremost Outsider Artists – artists who function outside the mainstream art community.

Outsider Artists often do not think of themselves as 'artists' or their work as 'art', and this fascinates those people who do. Since artists like Picasso and Duchamp reimagined what 'art' might be, artists have looked for inspiration to those who produce art naively and naturally: children, people living in what would have been considered (at the time the term Art Brut was first coined) 'primitive' societies, and the long-term mentally ill.

As time has gone by, the term has come to seem more problematic, especially in terms of the cultural appropriation of techniques and images from less developed countries by artists working in a lucrative Western art world. But it remains true that both children and some people with significant mental health conditions achieve a spontaneity and naturalness in their work that trained artists can't match but would dearly love to.

It was in this spirit that Bowie and Eno visited Gugging in the 1990s.

When they arrived, they had to walk through the main clinic on their way to the area where the artists lived and worked, and as they did so they were shocked to see graffiti on the wall that read 'THIS IS HELL'. In stark contrast to this, the artists' wing was decorated with the patients' own work, including murals depicting trees and other nature scenes.

Bowie said that what fascinated him at Gugging was the sense of exploration and the complete lack of self-judgement. As someone who was often undermined by self-criticism, he wanted to be able to create with that same judgement-free sense of innocence. In discussing his trips to Gugging, Bowie concluded that achieving this would be incredibly difficult but that 'it could be done'. The key, he felt, was a sense of play – a childlike freedom from criticism and fear – and his various randomizing techniques were designed to nurture this.

THE DIVIDED MIND

Bowie's fascination with the Gugging Artists and Outsider Art resonated strongly with the ideas expounded in a landmark book he was reading in the 1970s: the philosopher Julian Jaynes's *The Origin of Consciousness in the Breakdown of the Bicameral Mind*. This book was a revolutionary attempt to explain how consciousness evolved, how our minds had come to work in the way they do. Jaynes's theory was that until relatively recently our brain was bicameral – that is, the two hemispheres of our brain operated separately.

In ordinary life, the left side of the brain handled things, but at times of stress – at times when someone was struggling to know what to do – their right hemisphere spoke to the left hemisphere, giving it instructions on how to act. People perceived these utterances of the right hemisphere as coming from *outside* themselves. They were taken to be the commands of the gods and they were meant to be obeyed without question. We see this illustrated in ancient Greek literature, where characters have no conscious minds in the way that we understand the term now – no sense of inner introspection. They wait to be instructed by the gods, and when a god speaks, they have to follow the instructions. To disobey the voice of the gods is to court disaster.

Jaynes suggested the two hemispheres of the brain started to work more collaboratively only a little over three thousand years ago. It's a highly controversial theory. One criticism of Jaynes's work focuses on the belief that the three-thousand-year time span is too short for such a major evolution to have taken place.

But even if we dispute the timing of Jaynes's theory, and even if we question the theory itself, we can see how the idea would have fascinated Bowie as it offers further insight into schizophrenia and its disturbing symptom of hearing voices. If we believe Jaynes, we see that, until relatively recently, *all of us* heard voices; in which case, those suffering from schizophrenia are – under extreme trauma – effectively reverting to an old way of thinking.

It also raises the intriguing thought that, when artists use randomizing techniques in their quest for self-discovery, they too are reverting to an older way of using the mind: listening to and obeying the commands of 'the gods'.

YOU ARE A DISGRUNTLED EX-MEMBER OF THE CLASH

Like Bowie, Eno was heavily influenced by John Cage and was particularly fascinated by Cage's randomizing techniques that involved setting up a series of very clear conditions at the beginning of a piece and then allowing the music to 'write itself' within those boundaries. Along with the painter Peter Schmidt, Eno developed 'Oblique Strategies', a series of cards that were to be used whenever the composer or artist was stuck. He or she then simply pulled a card at random and did whatever it said. Once again, it's a technique that questions the idea of the artist as the conscious creator of the work, and seems to link back to the days of the bicameral mind, with the voice of the gods replaced by an instruction on a piece of card.

Working with Bowie on the 1970s trilogy of 'Berlin' albums – *Low*, *Heroes* and *Lodger* – Eno often used the Oblique Strategies cards. For Bowie's *1. Outside* album in the mid-1990s, Eno created new flashcards, showing one to each member of the band as a guide to how they should play on a given track. They said things like, 'You are a disgruntled ex-member of The Clash – play all the notes they wouldn't let you play.' Eno himself, meanwhile, had a radio at his side, which he would turn on randomly, sample and then add the sampled sound into the mix. At the same time, Bowie was surrounded by magazines and books, which he was cutting up and repurposing into lyrics, using the Dadaist/Beat technique.

WHAT IF?

At his commencement address to students at Berklee College of Music in 1999 Bowie said he quickly realized when he was learning to play the saxophone that he would not pursue natural expression in his work. Instead, he said, his art would be 'the game of "what if?"'

This was the game he played to try to manifest that 'something' inside himself, the game he played in pursuit of self-knowledge, the game he played to discover his higher being.

How can a game of 'what if?' – even one extended over a nearly fifty-year career – help someone discover their true self? The clue lies in the word 'game'. In visiting Gugging, Bowie was looking for a childlike innocence in the act of creation; in playing with scissors and bits of paper, he was emulating childhood play as much as he was fitting into an avant-garde tradition.

In doing all of this, Bowie was trying to shut down his thinking mind and return to a place before conceptual thought.

We could define 'a place before conceptual thought' as early childhood: before we learn to talk, before we attach language to objects, we think in a freer way. Or we could define it as the time before our bicameral mind joined together – a time when our whole species simply acted without constant introspection because introspection was not yet possible.

We could also see 'a place before conceptual thought' as one of the primary goals that Bowie's Buddhist studies and reading of Jung had been pointing him towards all along – a way to escape the 'micro-world inside of himself' and connect with his higher being. Jung stated that intellectual effort alone would not be enough to help the individual realize their true self. Buddhism goes one step further, suggesting that thought is an obstacle to truly understanding who you are and your place in the world.

To explore this 'place before thought' we'll spend a little more time with John Cage because Cage's journey was extremely similar to Bowie's (although occurring twenty years earlier), and in his lectures and essays Cage left a very clear trail behind him of what he was thinking and who he had been influenced by.

THE LIFE LESSON: CHANGE YOUR RELATIONSHIP WITH YOUR THOUGHTS

Conventionally we use our thinking mind to solve our problems. But sometimes our thoughts themselves can be the problem. Whether you are on a spiritual quest to connect with your true self or whether you simply want to find greater peace of mind, reframing your relationship with your thoughts is a vital step.

For most people John Cage is famous for *4'33'*, his 1952 composition that consists of four minutes and thirty-three seconds of silence. To some people it is a revolutionary reinvention of what music can be, and a profound meditation on what silence really is; to others, it's an object of bemusement, ridicule or scorn. Even Cage's mother, speaking to the composer Earle Brown at one performance, asked: 'Now, Earle, don't you think that John has gone too far this time?'

One person who attended the first performance of *4'33'* in Woodstock wrote a letter to the local paper, declaring that the piece was part of 'a war' that artists of the time were carrying out against 'common sense'. It was meant as a criticism. It is, in fact, entirely true. Cage *was* trying to attack common sense.

4'33' was a culmination of a process of discovery that began in 1939. When Cage attended the Cornish School in Seattle that year, he heard a talk by Nancy Wilson Ross, a novelist and expert on Eastern religions, who illuminated for him the connection between Dada and Zen. Cage had been struggling both as a person and as a composer, trying to find tranquillity in a tortured life, and also to find a purpose for his art: who was he and what was he here for? Inspired by this talk, he painstakingly built answers to these questions over the next decade and a half, finding his answers in Eastern philosophy.

As part of this journey, Cage read the works of the ninth-century Zen master Huang Po, where he encountered the idea that thought, rather than being a tool to solve life's problems, could indeed *be* the problem:

> If you wish to understand, know that a sudden comprehension comes when the mind has been purged of all the clutter of conceptual and discriminatory thought-activity. Those who seek the truth by means of intellect and learning only get further and further away from it. Not till your thoughts cease all their branching here and there, not till you abandon all thoughts of seeking for something, not till your mind is motionless as wood or stone, will you be on the right road.

Then in 1950, he discovered Daisetsu Teitaro Suzuki's books on Zen Buddhism teachings, and these seem to have brought a clear focus to all his study of Eastern religions, leaving Cage with a clear action plan for how he should live his life and how he should create his art.

Suzuki, like Huang Po, questions the value of thought. In his book *An Introduction to Zen Buddhism* (for which, aptly enough, Carl Jung wrote the foreword) Suzuki challenges the reader: 'Are you going to be eternally chained by your own laws of thought, or are you going to be perfectly free?'

Suzuki goes further, stating that, 'as long as one is conscious of space and time, Zen will always keep a respectable distance from you'. The implication is that our troubles began when, as Jaynes would have it, our bicameral minds broke down and we began to be conscious of our thoughts. Once we became aware of our thoughts, they started causing us problems.

Zen has its own unique form of training: the koan. Even if you know nothing of Zen you are probably aware of at least one koan: 'What is the sound of one hand clapping?' Zen students are given a koan like this to solve, but they are not really supposed to *solve* it because the koan has no solution. It doesn't make sense. It isn't meant to make sense.

Koans are, indeed, a war against common sense. They are meant to illustrate the limits of our sense, to show that our world of words, thoughts and concepts is not quite as useful or important as we conventionally think it is. Koans point to another way of being in which we hold our thoughts, our sense and our logic much more lightly.

DON'T BE LIKE A DOG, BE LIKE A LION

Milarepa was a Tibetan Buddhist master of the eleventh century and an important figure in the Kagyu lineage. He had a very similar view on how we should treat our thoughts to Huang Po and Suzuki, but he expressed it in a more engaging way: 'When you run after your thoughts, you are like a dog chasing a stick: every time a stick is thrown, you run after it. Instead, be like a lion who, rather than chasing after the stick, turns to face the thrower. One only throws a stick at a lion once.'

If that.

As you have been experiencing the meditations and the exercises in this book, you may have already gained a sense of what Milarepa is talking about. The instruction you're given – to focus on the breath – is so simple. Yet, inevitably, thoughts arise and distract you. And even though, before you start meditating, you know that your task is to let the thoughts go and bring the attention back to the breath, once the thought has hooked you this is remarkably difficult to do.

But what's wrong with this, really? Why did Milarepa, Huang Po, Suzuki and of course the Buddha himself all warn against following our thoughts?

To understand this, we have to look more closely at what thoughts actually are and at the harm they can do us.

The question 'What is thought?' is a complex one, but the form of thought we are most often aware of – and that appears to be one of the forms of thought the wise masters warn us against – is our inner speech: the strange commentary that runs in our head almost incessantly. I say 'strange' but it doesn't seem strange to us as long as we're lost in it. It's just how life is. It's how life has always been. But when you stop and observe it, it *does* seem to be strange. You start to wonder what it's actually *for*.

Not everyone thinks in exactly the same way, but most of you reading this now will be 'hearing' your inner voice read the book to you. Your inner voice is, as it were, reading the book aloud to you in your head. As I write these words I am also 'saying' them to myself in my head.

Some people experience this inner speech as a monologue. It's as if they are talking to themselves, but it's all happening in their head. Other people experience it more as a dialogue: they ask themselves questions and then answer them. Occasionally, they 'hear' these voices as being slightly different. They have a play going on in their head with different characters. Some people augment their inner speech with visual imagery, 'seeing' images in their head.

We use this inner-speech form of thinking to help us in several ways. We use it when we're planning and when we're reflecting on past events. We use it both to motivate ourselves and to criticize ourselves.

When we stop and think about this, it definitely seems strange. Why are we commenting on the world to ourselves, instead of simply experiencing the world? What is the point of telling ourselves what is happening and what we are doing when, surely, we already know because we are the ones doing it? And here lies one of the key problems with thought that the ancient traditions warn us about: it keeps us almost permanently at one remove from life.

WHAT'S SO WRONG WITH THINKING?

Our thoughts separate us from reality

We spend our whole lives telling ourselves what's happening to us with our inner speech – as if we weren't already aware. It's as though, instead of playing a sport, we've decided to live in the commentators' box, accompanied by a pundit who tends to have a very negative view of the game that is happening, and of our performance in it.

In Chapter 1 we discussed those rare and wonderful moments that we describe with the phrase 'I never felt more alive.' These are the moments when our inner speech turns off, when we come face to face with reality instead of living it through this layer of commentary. It feels amazing. And yet, for 99.9 per cent of our lives, we keep the commentary running – diluting our experience of being alive. But if living without it is so amazing, why don't we turn it off more often? Because it's extremely difficult to make it cease.

We can't turn our thoughts off

Psychologists talk about 'the resting state of the brain' to describe what the brain does when it is not focused on completing a specific task that will require attention. But in this task-negative state, the brain isn't really resting at all. It just keeps chattering away.

This chatter tends to consist of a moment-to-moment commentary on what is happening around us, supplemented with a great deal of judgement on whether we like it or not. Our 'resting state' also includes mental time travel that takes us out of the present moment, either to look back at the past or to look forward.

Our thoughts can be unnecessary and unhelpful

Sometimes when the masters of the ancient wisdom traditions talk about how we need to get rid of thought, it's easy to get confused. After all, thinking is one of our most powerful tools, and much of it is really useful. We can usefully remember Bowie's teacher Chime Rinpoche and his more accessible way of discussing the issue. He says the problem is '*unnecessary* thoughts'.

Perhaps, for many of us, reaching a Zen-like state when our mind is, as Huang Po put it, 'motionless as wood or stone' seems impossible. But if we can rid ourselves of (or, at least, reduce) our unnecessary and unhelpful thoughts, we can be much less stressed and much happier.

Unnecessary thoughts are pretty easy to spot: they're any thoughts that aren't helpful. The classic example of an unnecessary thought has been experienced by anyone with an office job on the night before a big meeting. You wake up at 3 a.m. After a few moments, you realize this isn't one of those roll-over-and-go-back-to-sleep moments. This is an I'm-going-to-be-lying-awake-staring-at-the-ceiling-for-quite-a-while moment. You have your first unnecessary thought: 'I really need to get back to sleep.'

It's unnecessary – and unhelpful – because no one ever got back to sleep by thinking that they needed to get back to sleep. In fact, as you no doubt know, thinking about how you *have* to get back to sleep invariably makes it *harder* to get back to sleep. As you lie awake, you soon have a series of further unnecessary and unhelpful thoughts:

> 'I hope I don't screw up in the meeting.'
>
> 'If I don't get to sleep soon, I will definitely screw up.'
>
> 'I always do this before every big meeting. I lay awake, and then I'm a wreck in the meeting.'
>
> 'What's the matter with me? Why do I sabotage myself like this?'

Not everyone's stream of unnecessary thoughts is exactly like that, but you'll recognize the pattern. What we need our thinking mind to do for us is help us relax and get back to sleep; what it actually does for us is make us more stressed, ensuring we stay awake.

Your thoughts at times like this are unnecessary and can be unhelpful. Some of our thoughts are much worse than this.

Many of our thoughts are positively harmful to us

In our 'lying awake at night' scenario, it seems as though our thoughts are almost teasing us. For many of us, our thoughts can sometimes seem more like bullies or abusers.

For people with anxiety, a slight unease can be accelerated into a panic attack by a vicious spiral of thinking.

For those with OCD, their unwanted thoughts can control their actions. For some this occurs at a level that is merely slightly irritating, but for others their lives can be paralyzed by ritualistic behaviour, all driven by intrusive thoughts.

For those with depression, a succession of sad or negative thoughts can trigger or worsen their depressed state.

And millions of people who would not identify as having any mental health problems go through life with low self-esteem and a sometimes brutal inner critic, plagued by constant self-critical thoughts that can sabotage relationships, jobs and lives. They're so used to this they consider it normal.

In one sense, it seems almost too glaringly obvious to make the point that our thoughts contribute to all this misery. But it needs to be stated clearly because some of us are so trapped in the world of thought that we don't realize that's where we are. We're so completely identified with our thoughts that we don't realize we are not our thoughts.

It is vitally important to really understand this point because knowing that your thoughts contribute to so much of your suffering means you can act to reduce your suffering by simply changing your relationship with your thoughts.

The first step towards changing your relationship with your thoughts, is simply to understand that you *have* a relationship with your thoughts. And that involves being very clear that your thoughts are not you.

YOUR PATH

In this section you will learn that you are not your thoughts, and then use that knowledge to change your relationship with your thoughts for the better. If you are plagued with negative thoughts or a vicious 'inner critic' the techniques we explore here can bring relief, but they are also helpful for anyone who seeks to truly understand who they are and how they relate to the world.

In one of her talks the inspirational mindfulness teacher Tara Brach tells her audience she is going to share with them the three most valuable lessons in the world. She reveals the first one: 'Don't believe your thoughts.'

There is a hushed expectancy in the audience as she prepares to reveal the second one. She speaks: 'Don't believe your thoughts.'

The audience laughs. And, of course they now know what the third one is going to be: 'Don't believe your thoughts.'

It's a vital lesson. Or perhaps it's three vital lessons. But before you can choose to not believe your thoughts, there's one other thing you need to learn. So I would argue that the three most valuable lessons in the world are actually these:

1. You are not your thoughts.

2. You are not your thoughts.
3. You are not your thoughts.

What does that really mean?

Well, thoughts are part of you. They're going on inside you. But they do not define you. They are not the essence of you. You are something much bigger than your thoughts.

So what *are* you?

In the meditations we have been doing, you have been instructed to notice your thoughts. You are the thing that *notices* the thoughts. You are that *awareness*.

If that's still a slightly tricky concept, let's take it outside of your body for a moment.

Are you this book? (I promise you it's not a trick question.) Are you the book you're reading right now? No, you're not. Are you aware of the book? Yes, you are. You are what is aware of the book. You can observe the book, but the fact that you can observe the book doesn't mean that you *are* the book. The book you are reading does not define you. That would just be silly.

Similarly, you can observe your thoughts, but the fact that you can observe your thoughts doesn't mean that you *are* your thoughts. Your thoughts do not define you. That would be equally silly.

You may object to this. You may think the book and your thoughts are not the same kind of thing. You may say, 'The book is just here, but I generate my thoughts.' But when we meditate, we learn this isn't exactly true. Many of our thoughts are not generated by us – or certainly not consciously generated by us. They just happen inside us. Many of them, we don't even want. Many of them are not relevant, useful or helpful – or even true. They just go on happening.

When we understand that we are not our thoughts, we are practising what psychologists refer to as 'cognitive defusion' – a vital skill both in tackling mental health issues and in increasing self knowledge and self understanding.

To get a closer look at the difference between thoughts and *awareness* of thoughts, let's meditate again.

Exercise: You are not your thoughts

Close your eyes.

Take three deep, slow breaths.

Focus your attention on the breath. With each in breath, breathe in a sense of space. As you breathe out, relax.

Now focus your attention in your body. Focus on the sensations in your body. Just scan through your body, noticing what is going on right now.

Which part of your body are you most aware of? Why? Is it tense? Tight? Relaxed? Hot? Cold?

As you observe the sensations, do they change? Take some time to simply notice what is occurring in your body. As long as you like.

As you do this, be aware *of your awareness*. Notice that *you* are *observing* all this. You have a body. But you are not your body. You are the observer.

Now, from this same place of awareness, observe your thoughts.

Focus on the internal conversation we all have with ourselves. It might be going: 'What's all this about being aware of awareness?' Or: 'Of course I'm my thoughts,' or: 'I'm not having any thoughts yet – so I can't observe them.' Those are all thoughts. Every day you have thousands of thoughts. Some of them are useful. Some of them are pointless. But they continue relentlessly.

Now let the thoughts go and return your focus to your breath.

Within moments thoughts will occur again. They might be: 'Great, I'm totally focused on my breath.' Or: 'I'm not having any thoughts at all,' or: 'He's wrong, you know. My mind is completely blank right now.' These are all thoughts. Notice them. Notice that you don't make them happen. They just happen on their own.

Again, be aware *of your awareness*. Notice that *you* are *observing* all this. You have thoughts. But you are not your thoughts. You are the observer of your thoughts.

Notice that, by observing your bodily sensations or your thoughts, you can become aware of yourself as pure awareness. As the observer of all these experiences.

You have a body, you have thoughts. But you are not these things. You are the pure awareness that observes them.

This is who you are. For much of our lives, many of us are so lost in thought that we never really see through our thoughts to connect with who we actually are. Usually when we do, there is a sense of space, of light, of calm or of peace. If you are experiencing this, stay with it for as long as you like.

Then, when you are ready, turn your attention outside your body, to the sounds in the room. Focus on those for a few moments.

Wiggle your fingers and toes.

Then slowly, in your own time, open your eyes.

In all my training and coaching work, helping people to understand that 'you are not your thoughts' is one of the two most transformative moments. (The other is the REAL meditation, which we will encounter in Chapter 7.)

It is a Matrix moment. Just as Neo in the film *The Matrix* learns that the reality he has lived in his whole life isn't reality at all, we learn that this world of our thoughts is not quite as real as we think it is. Reality is what happens when our thoughts stop for a moment and we have a direct experience of the world itself unfiltered by our commentary and judgement.

Of course, your thoughts are real. They're happening. But the world they create if you completely identify with them and believe them isn't quite as real as you think. It's a version of the world that has been heavily modified by your thoughts.

How shall we use this knowledge? By endeavouring to hold our thoughts a little more lightly going forward – by gently questioning and challenging them on occasion. By knowing that whenever we want we can find that space between our self and our thoughts through meditation.

When you're new to the realization that you are not your thoughts, your grip on it can be a little shaky, but the more you meditate, the stronger your grasp of the concept will become. After you've practised observing your thoughts from this place of awareness within your meditation for a while, you will be able to take this skill out into the real world. Then, instead of being ruled by your thoughts, you will be able to notice them as they arise and to decide what to do with each one. You can ask yourself:

- Is this relevant to me?
- Is this true?
- Is this helpful?

If any of your thoughts are not relevant, true and helpful, you can choose to let them go. This may seem unlikely right now – especially if you are deeply affected by troubling thoughts – but, given time and practice, it is achievable.

If you're thinking, 'But how can my thoughts not be relevant to me? After all, *I'm* having them,' I think the most helpful analogy is to think of the ads you see on your computer screen and how they get there.

Let's imagine, for example, that you buy a mattress online. If you are like most people, you won't buy another mattress for about ten years. You are now not only in the category 'not going to buy a mattress' but you are also as far away from the 'about to buy a mattress' category as you could possibly be. However, the technology that serves you ads on your computer has registered that you are someone who is incredibly interested in mattresses and so it will continue to send you ads for mattresses for many months.

Now, it's not true to say that these ads have *nothing* to do with you. In fact, your behaviour is, in a sense, the reason these ads exist, but that does not make them relevant to you or helpful to you. Nor is their view of you – 'this is a person who really wants to find out about mattresses' – true. Just as these ads can be connected to your past and yet not be relevant, helpful or true right now, in a similar way your thoughts may be somehow connected to your past and yet be equally irrelevant, unhelpful and untrue in your present.

So please do not feel that you have to identify with your thoughts any more closely than you identify with the ads that pop up on your screen.

Exercise: Noticing and labelling thoughts (outside of meditation)

Sometimes people I have taught to meditate and who have appreciated the benefit of creating this slight sense of separation from their thoughts will ask me: 'But what do I do when I *can't* meditate? I can't meditate in real life.' Naturally I –

slightly annoyingly – point out that meditation *is* real life; in fact, it's arguably more real than their autopilot, day-to-day existence. But I know what they mean. They can't meditate in the middle of a busy meeting, when they're driving, when they're shopping, when they're out and about living their regular lives.

The good news is that, away from your meditation, you can practise various techniques that will increase cognitive defusion; that is, they will allow a little bit more space between your self and your thoughts.

In this way, you will strengthen your understanding that you are not your thoughts, thus:

- reducing the power of your thoughts to hurt you
- allowing you to spend more of your life directly experiencing the world and not 'lost in thought'
- helping you on your journey to understand who you truly are.

All of these techniques build on the ability to notice thoughts, which you've developed during the meditation.

The first technique is simply to notice and label your thoughts as they arise. This involves labelling the thought in a specific way that acknowledges you are not the thought you are having.

So if, for example, you forgot a friend's birthday and you found yourself thinking 'I am a bad friend', the first thing you need to do is simply notice that you are having the thought. The more you meditate, the more easily you will notice and identify thoughts *as thoughts* outside of meditation.

The next stage is to label the thought, for instance: 'I am currently observing that the thought "I am a bad friend" is occurring in my mind.' It's an unusual form of words. It's not how we normally talk – but this is important. We have replaced 'I am a bad friend' with 'I am currently observing that the thought "I am a bad friend" is occurring in my mind.' We've done this because 'I am a bad friend' leaves you completely identified with the thought. You *are* a bad friend – and there's no room to question or challenge this. On the other hand, 'I am currently observing that the thought "I am a bad friend" is occurring in my mind' is a form of words that identifies you as the observer of the thought. You are not identified with the thought. You are *not* the thought. You can question or challenge the thought. There is a world of difference between the two states.

Exercise: Questioning thoughts

Simply noticing and labelling can be enough to reduce the power of negative thoughts. With more upsetting negative thoughts you may wish to go further.

Let's continue with the same example. You have had the thought: 'I am a bad friend,' and you have reframed it using our labelling technique as: 'I am currently observing that the thought "I am a bad friend" is occurring in my mind.' Now that you are not completely identified with the thought – now that you have acknowledged it is a thought that you are observing – you can try asking a few questions.

Is it absolutely, 100 per cent definitely true? Of course, you would rather have remembered the birthday, but does forgetting a birthday once make you a bad friend? Is there any other evidence you can think of that actually you are sometimes a good friend to this person?

Is it always true? Are you always a bad friend? How do you treat your other friends? Can you find any evidence in other relationships that argues against concluding that you are 'a bad friend'?

Is there another way to look at the situation? What else is going on in your life right now that might explain why you forgot? Are you overloaded or under pressure? Is there any reason why you should show yourself a little compassion right now rather than being hard on yourself over one mistake?

What would you say to a friend of yours who had this thought? If you really cared about someone and they made one mistake, what would you say to them? Probably you would suggest they are a good person really, and a good friend, and that this one lapse didn't prove otherwise. You might also suggest an action plan for saying sorry to the friend whose birthday was forgotten – a gift, a treat, a handwritten note…

Exercise: Your top ten

If you notice that certain negative thoughts recur frequently, it can be helpful to rank them in a top five or top ten. Write it down. Put it on a wall. Then, when a particular thought comes along, label it: 'I am currently observing that thought number five is occurring in my mind.'

Using this phraseology adds another layer of cognitive defusion, and can allow you to examine even very negative thoughts within a framework of humour.

Exercise: Befriending your inner critic

This exercise is based on the counterintuitive assumption that your inner critic is your friend. For those who suffer with a particularly vicious inner critic, this may sound ridiculous. However, this approach has been helpful for many people, and it's worth exploring. The thinking behind it is that, although your inner critic is clearly not behaving in a friendly way, it is – deep down – trying to look after you. It just doesn't know how to do it.

You already know how powerful your inner critic is. This exercise allows you to harness that power to work *for* you instead of against you.

Next time you are aware of your inner critic offering you negative advice and judgement, begin a conversation with it. Ask your inner critic: 'Why are you here?'

Close your eyes, breathe slowly and wait for an answer.

If you don't get an answer, repeat the question.

You may need to add a more leading question. There are many things you could say. Any of these:

> 'I know you're trying to help me. How are you trying to help me?'
>
> 'What are you trying to do for me?'

> 'Thank you for trying to help me. But the approach you're taking is not very helpful. Is there another way you could help me?'
>
> 'What else could you do to help me?'
>
> 'I'd like us to work together on this, but we need to come out with a new way of working together. What could that be?'

You can put the question into language that works for you, as long as you ask it as a polite, friendly request for cooperation – not an attack.

If you've spent many years suffering with an inner critic, before you start this exercise it may seem absurd. But please try it. If you find you get nowhere with it, then instead use the *Questioning thoughts* techniques (above) to challenge your inner critic. But it's always worthwhile trying the *Befriending* approach first as it brings all the energy that resides within your inner critic onto 'your side'.

Your path: Going forward

1. Continue your meditation practice. Try to increase the length of time you are meditating, but not if this reduces the number of times you meditate. Frequency is key. As well as noticing your thoughts, notice that you are noticing your thoughts. Take every opportunity to strengthen your understanding that you are not your thoughts; you are the observer of your thoughts.

2. Even if the idea of saying to yourself things like 'I am currently observing that the thought "I am a bad friend" is occurring in my mind' seems completely absurd to you, try to do it for a few days (with whatever negative thought is occurring, obviously). With repetition it will come to seem normal (which it is) and simply thinking 'I am a bad friend' (or whatever the thought is) will come to seem incorrect (which it is).

3. Think about Bowie's 'small universes that can be created inside the mind'. What does this mean to you? What small universes have you created in your mind with your thoughts? Bowie said the alternative was to 'receive the whole world as [your] home'. What would that feel like?

4. Ask yourself: 'Who am I if I am not my thoughts?' When you meditate and you notice your thoughts, what does the bit of you that notices the thoughts feel like? How is it different from your thinking mind? How is it different from the self that you have been revealing to the rest of the world? I am not being funny when I say don't overthink these questions. Just stay with them. You don't have to come up with definitive answers. But live with the ideas for a week.

CHAPTER 6: HELL

The life lesson: Growth is always possible – even in our darkest times

That's the one thing that people really think: do I belong here? Who are my friends? Am I on my own? God, it's terrifying to be on your own in this world.

(Bowie, 1987)

When one creates phantoms for oneself one puts vampires into the world, and one must nourish these children of a voluntary nightmare with one's blood, one's life, one's intelligence and one's reason without ever satisfying them.

(Eliphas Levi)

Things get very clear when you're cornered.

(Chögyam Trungpa Rinpoche)

BOWIE'S PATH

In 1975 Bowie sank into a cocaine-fuelled, anorexic, psychotic breakdown. And yet, somehow, from the depths of his despair Bowie resolved to clean up his act, to discard his characters and to finally begin to confront reality.

On 29 May 2004, David Bowie stood on the stage of the Borgata Event Center in Atlantic City. His band had just finished playing 'Reality', the title track of his latest album. Bowie strode up to the mic to introduce the next song, 'Station to Station', the title track of one of his classic 1970s albums.

'This,' he said, 'is from back in the Seventies. Well, *my* Seventies. They weren't necessarily *your* Seventies.'

Bowie's friend and sometimes collaborator Lou Reed wrote – on the liner notes of his confrontational, avant-garde album *Metal Machine Music* – the arrogant claim that 'my week beats your year', and surely many of those in the audience in Atlantic City would have assumed Bowie's statement was along similar boastful lines: he was a globally acclaimed creative genius, and they probably weren't.

But, as we've already discovered in earlier chapters, this was not how Bowie viewed 'his' 1970s – certainly not the period in which he wrote and recorded 'Station to Station'. Bowie's *internal*

1970s were not at all similar to the way the rest of the world saw him at the time.

Bowie described the period from the end of 1974 through to the first half of 1976 (the period when he broke America with the number-one hit 'Fame', gave the best acting performance of his life in the film *The Man Who Fell to Earth* and recorded 'Station to Station') as the darkest days of his life.

For much of this period, he was holed up in Los Angeles, a city he detested, living as a recluse. He stayed originally with Deep Purple bassist Glenn Hughes, then moved in with his business advisor Michael Lippman. After spending three months filming *The Man Who Fell to Earth* in New Mexico, he then returned to LA to rent a house in Bel Air.

Lippman later remembered 'dramatically erratic behaviour… he would not come out of his house… He was overworked and under a lot of pressure and unable to accept the realities of certain facts.' This assessment of the situation is something of an understatement. Never mind 'certain facts', Bowie was struggling to keep hold of any grasp of reality at all. For him these were days of psychological terror.

He was anorexic, weighing something like ninety-five pounds: 'not even skin and bone. I was just bone – bone with these veins wrapped around.' He would joke later that the only benefit of fame that he could think of – the ability to get a table at a fashionable restaurant – was useless to him since he ate nothing, subsisting on milk.

Fuelled by cocaine, he worked for days on end (allegedly even Keith Richards was shocked by his ability to go without sleep) as he wrote music, painted, sculpted and read obsessively, delving deep into the study of arcane and esoteric subjects. Doubtless the anorexia, lack of sleep and his prodigious cocaine consumption contributed to his fragile mental state.

Rumours of Bowie's behaviour during this period fill the more lurid biographies of him. He was convinced that both human beings and demons were trying to kill him. To deal with the former, he kept a gun in the house; to deal with the latter, he drew pentagrams on many surfaces. He kept his toenail clippings and his urine to prevent them being used in magic spells against him. He hired a white witch, Walli Elmlark, to perform an exorcism of the pool at the Bel Air house, which he was convinced had become possessed by an evil spirit.

We also know from Bowie's own testimony that the characters he had created in the previous years, and which he had tried in vain to 'kill off', now became intensely and frighteningly real for him – malignant forces that appeared as hallucinations, threatening him and telling him they had come to take him over completely. Bowie believed he was finally about to fall over the edge of the precipice that he had feared since his half-brother's breakdown. He later recalled thinking:

> 'This is it, Terry. I'm just about to join you.'

We are left with an image that seems psychologically eerily similar (albeit physically the complete opposite) of Marlon Brando's Colonel Kurtz in *Apocalypse Now*: a lone figure hiding from the world, thought by others to be powerful but in fact now a mere shell, his sanity crumbling, his world collapsing, quietly moaning 'the horror, the horror'.

IS ANYBODY OUT THERE?

There have been other rock stars who have suffered drug-fuelled psychotic breakdowns, but Bowie's experience was different in two important ways: first, in terms of his work; second, in terms of the outcome.

Usually if any work at all is produced by artists during these episodes, it is sketchy, unfinished and distinctly sub-par; yet somehow, in the midst of this desperate breakdown, Bowie was able to make a masterpiece: his *Station to Station* album.

Unsurprisingly, two of the songs on *Station to Station* – the title track and 'Word on a Wing' – are desperate cries for help.

'Word on a Wing' is essentially a prayer. It's not a conventional prayer, though; it is, as the author Chris O'Leary put it, more of 'an opening negotiation'. Bowie, sizing up God, makes it clear in a hopelessly untruthful display of bravado that he doesn't need any help right now, that actually he's frightfully busy, but that if God *really* wants to talk then he'll see if he can fit something in the diary.

In contrast, 'Station to Station' is a deep dive into the mystical Kabbalah and the Western magical tradition that built upon it, including the Hermetic Order of the Golden Dawn and the work of Aleister Crowley (the English ceremonial magician who was once called 'the wickedest man in the world'). Bowie has referred to it as a 'magical treatise'.

In the song, Bowie is at one point adrift and isolated, as we know he was at the time, but then he refers to moving from Keter to Malkhut – two of the sephirot (points on the tree) on the Kabbalistic Tree of Life – a manoeuvre that implies godlike powers of creation.

While the phrase 'station to station' might refer literally to a railway journey (Bowie's preferred means of travel) and might also refer to the Stations of the Cross, it's worth remembering that – at the time the album was written – the phrase could also refer to a particular type of phone call.

Back in the days when households shared one landline and phone calls were often placed via an operator, you could ask for a 'person to person' call; with this kind of call if it was answered but the individual you wanted to speak to was not present, you didn't have to pay for the call. Alternatively, you could ask for a 'station to station' call where, if the phone call connected you paid for it, *whoever* answered.

Bowie, unable or unwilling to sleep, had been sitting alone in his Bel Air hideaway, devouring texts on Christian Gnosticism, Kabbalah, magic, alchemy, numerology, tarot – even the Nazi search for the Holy Grail. These are the ingredients that fed *Station to Station*. They were also the avenues he was exploring as he sought a way out of his psychological torment.

Whether we see them as a reading list or hear them combined in a song, it's hard to escape the sense that Bowie was putting a station to station call out to the world and didn't really care who answered it. Anyone or anything that could help him lock his characters out of his life, tame his demons, silence the voices, end his hallucinations and offer him a path back to sanity was welcome to pick up the phone.

BACK FROM THE BRINK

This brings us to the second way Bowie's psychotic breakdown was different from those experienced by some other rock stars (and by Terry): he recovered. Bowie returned not just to a semblance of his former health but in fact he became physically, mentally and emotionally stronger than before. How did he manage this?

Mick Ronson, the talented guitarist who had been so important in the development of Bowie's Ziggy Stardust-era sound, was interviewed in 1975 and asked about his former collaborator. 'What he really needs is some good friends around him,' said the caring but no-nonsense Ronson. 'I just wish he could be in this room right now, sat here, so I could kick some sense into him.'

That was never going to happen. Bowie had severed ties with just about everyone who had helped make him famous or who might offer him support at this time. Fortunately for Bowie, he had one friend left – his PA, Coco Schwab – who did (more or less) what Ronson wanted to do. Dragging him in front of a mirror and forcing him to look at his wasted self, she told Bowie that if he carried on as he was, even she would leave him. 'You're not worth the effort,' she said.

As a threat it was quite possibly not true; Schwab was fiercely loyal to Bowie throughout his life. But as a challenge, as a provocation – did *Bowie himself* think he was worth the effort? – it was extremely successful.

Bowie responded by leaving the hollow, showbiz world of LA and went to Switzerland, staying there only briefly before deciding to live in Berlin. There, instead of his lavish but closeted rock-star lifestyle, he stayed in (relatively) modest surroundings. Instead of sitting in a room and having everything brought to him, he went out into the real world and learned to re-engage with life. He began to put himself back together again.

It's clearly not an adequate explanation to suggest that Coco Schwab had saved Bowie by telling him to get his act together. We all know that telling an addict or someone suffering from anorexia or experiencing psychotic delusions to 'pull yourself together' is almost certainly not going to effect any change. We also know that the advice given to anyone trying to kick a drug habit would be to distance themselves from their addict friends. In direct contravention of this advice, Bowie took fellow addict Iggy Pop to Berlin with him so that they could help each other recover.

He had no psychiatric help. This was many years before he tried a twelve-step program. He had the 'bad influence' of Iggy Pop right by his side. And yet, somehow, he was able to claw himself back from anorexia and psychosis, and also to better manage (although not rid himself of) his addictions. This is a level of recovery that many are unable to achieve, even with intensive psychiatric care and powerful medication.

Although he still had a long road of recovery ahead of him, the progress that Bowie made in the later stages of 1976 and in 1977 was remarkable. We have to conclude, therefore, that the work he did on himself – the studying, reflection and contemplation – helped give him the resources and the resilience he needed to do this; that hidden behind the rumoured weirdness and excesses of his time in LA, Bowie was working hard to reclaim his sanity; that within the strange collection of philosophies, religions and cultish beliefs that he explored in his Bel Air hideaway, he found enough truth and enough support to help him climb out of the abyss.

In the next section we will look at these philosophies or religions, belief systems and ancient traditions. But rather than look at them for shock value (urine in the fridge!), we will explore the wisdom underpinning them, look at how they connect with each other, and how they relate to (and differ from) Bowie's core Buddhist and Jungian perspective.

We will explore how they might have helped Bowie, and how the truths within them can also help us when we encounter life's most difficult passages.

THE LIFE LESSON: GROWTH IS ALWAYS POSSIBLE – EVEN IN OUR DARKEST TIMES

Many of us get lost at some point on our journey through life: a major depression, a breakdown, a midlife crisis. Sometimes from our hardest struggles come our most important learnings. How can the eclectic group of esoteric teachings that Bowie turned to at his lowest point guide us through our own 'dark night of the soul'?

During the mid-1960s, David Bowie and Marc Bolan were friends and rivals.

When Bolan's band Tyrannosaurus Rex played a show at London's Royal Festival Hall in June 1968, Bolan invited Bowie to be his support act, but only on the condition that he didn't play any songs.

This condition might sound strange, but it wasn't a problem for Bowie at the time. He had already released nine major-label singles by this time, and each one of them had been a flop. It's hardly surprising, then, that he was seriously considering giving up his plans to be a pop star, and had trained as a mime artist with Lindsay Kemp. He agreed to support Bolan by staging a twenty-minute solo mime piece called *Jetsun and the Eagle*.

The Jetsun of the title was Jetsun Milarepa. As you will recall from Chapter 5, Milarepa is the wise man who told us not to chase our thoughts in the way a dog chases a stick, but rather to be like a lion. One of the reasons Milarepa is so important is that he embodies a key principle of the Kagyu lineage of Buddhism: that anyone, no matter what their situation, can achieve enlightenment – and that this transformation can be achieved in one lifetime, without the need for the countless reincarnations that we read about in the more mythical strands of the religion.

When Milarepa's father died, his mother was tricked out of her inheritance by Milarepa's aunt and uncle. His mother encouraged Milarepa to take revenge and he killed his aunt's entire family. Later, racked with guilt and sorrow, he became a student of the Buddhist master Marpa and, after a long period of redemptive physical labour, he achieved enlightenment and became a wise teacher.

Milarepa's story has been used frequently in teachings by Chögyam Trungpa Rinpoche and Chime Rinpoche, and their student Bowie was fascinated by him. Milarepa's story tells us that, no matter what situation you are in, no matter how hopeless you feel, no matter how many mis-steps you may have made in your life, no matter how far you have fallen, you can turn things round, grow and develop, and find new purpose in your life.

In fact, our darkest days often lead directly to personal transformation.

CRISIS OR OPPORTUNITY?

What happened to Bowie in 1975 looks like a complete collapse. However, we could reframe it as a vital step on a particularly difficult spiritual journey.

When we encounter similarly difficult periods in our own lives, it is possible to see things in these terms but it usually becomes much easier to see them in this way many years after the event. Once we have climbed out of the abyss, we have the perspective to look back, recognize what we learned from the experience and how it shaped and enhanced our later life, and then – and only then – we may be grateful for it. At the time, however, the last thing it feels like is 'an opportunity for growth'.

We might think of the experience as a breakdown, we might call it a midlife crisis, and if we are religious we might call it a crisis of faith. In Jungian terms we could suggest that it is the moment when our persona has become so far removed from our self that it is simply no longer sustainable. Perhaps we might call it our 'dark night of the soul'. However we describe it, our old ways of functioning don't work any more; we need to find a new way of functioning or…

We may not even know what the 'or' is, because this can be a time of utter despair. There is no joy in life. There is no meaning. You begin to question why you are here. You may question more widely the life you have been living. You lose interest even in those things that you were previously passionate about. You become aware of the limits of your power to control the world around you. You predominantly feel negative emotions, such as anger, sadness, frustration – often without knowing why. You feel that other people cannot possibly understand what you're going through. You may underneath all this have a strong sense of shame or worthlessness. Your experience might feel a lot like grief, even though you may not have lost anybody.

In psychological terms it seems a lot like depression. This may be how you or your doctor come to define it.

If you are turning to this chapter specifically because you are going through a very difficult time right now and are looking for guidance, you would be forgiven for being a little bit cynical or even suspicious. What's this? Alchemy? Magic? Kabbalah? On the surface, it doesn't sound like the obvious path, does it? But we need to remember three things.

First, Bowie got better. Somewhere in the esoteric subjects he studied during this period, and in the wisdom he had already gleaned from his Buddhist studies and his reading of Jung, he found enough clues to stage a remarkable physical, mental and emotional recovery.

Second, behind the sometimes bizarre and off-putting language and rituals of these practices lie millennia of wisdom. It can be hard to pinpoint but, at the core of this complex and esoteric wisdom, steeped in allegory, metaphor and deliberate obfuscation, lie potentially helpful teachings.

Third, we are looking at these areas only as one element for you to consider within the wider mix of teachings elsewhere in this book – and any other support you might seek (see page 207). You will, as ever, pick what works for you.

Our purpose is to uncover the wisdom that guided Bowie through life. At this stage, the ideas he chose to explore were extremely esoteric and arcane. We're going to follow him along this path. It can be complex; it can involve rethinking some concepts; it can be easy to feel a bit lost. Don't worry, we're not going to disappear too far down the rabbit holes. And when we have found our way through Gnosticism, the Kabbalah, alchemy and magic, we will regroup on the other side and analyze what we have learned and how it can help us.

At no point will you be made to wear funny hats, convert to a new religion, cast spells or join any secret societies. When we look at Gnosticism, the Kabbalah, alchemy and magic, we will find that:

> they do not say what most people imagine they say
>
> in fact, they say something *completely* different from what most people imagine they say
>
> they converge around a few core ideas, which are in essence very similar to the ideas we have discovered in Buddhism and in Jungian psychology.

They were begun by human beings trying to answer exactly the same questions we are trying to answer today. Who am I? What is my place in the world? How can I bring meaning to my life?

DON'T LET GOD GET IN YOUR WAY

As we explore Gnosticism and Kabbalah, we will once again encounter the God barrier: most of us these days don't believe in God, so how can we learn anything from traditions that are all about God? Fortunately, this isn't really a problem because within these traditions, the word 'God' does not mean what most people think it does.

When Gnostics or Kabbalists talk about God, they do not mean a bloke with a white beard who lives in the sky. That's not God at all. People who think of God like that are 'fools' according to Rabbi Moshe Cordovero, a great Kabbalist teacher of the sixteenth century.

Some Gnostics go further, saying that not only did the God of the Old Testament *not* create us but in fact *we* created *him*. Therefore he embodies many of our worst attributes as well as our better side; the Gnostic Bishop Rosamonde Miller wrote, 'Human beings, being flawed, projected a mixture of all their self-hatred as well as their loftiest aspirations even to a being they called God.'

When Kabbalists talk of God, they talk of Ein Sof. This is the infinite, indescribable power that underpins all existence. In fact, it *is* all of existence. Like Buddhists and other Eastern religions, Kabbalists reject dualism – the idea that we're all separate, the idea that there is 'you' and 'the rest of the world', and that 'you' are separate from 'it'. There is only Ein Sof – being, existence – and we're all it. We are all connected and we are all 'God'.

So you are God, but don't get carried away – so is everybody and every*thing* else. This book is God, but so is every other book.

Cordovero wrote: 'The essence of divinity is found in every single thing – nothing but it exists. Since it causes every thing to be, no thing can live by anything else... Ein Sof exists in each existent. Do not say, "This is a stone and not God." God forbid! Rather, all existence is God, and the stone is a thing pervaded by divinity.'

It's not an easy idea to get our heads around because we *seem* so separate; for now, let's perhaps proceed with it as a thought experiment: let's just work on the basis that it *might* be true and see where that takes us.

When Gnostics and Kabbalists talk of getting closer to God, they don't mean that we will find ourselves sitting by the side of an old white-bearded man on a throne in the sky. They mean that we may get just a glimpse of how the universe really works, that we might start to see through the illusion of our dualistic 'reality' and start to uncover who we truly are.

As you read through the rest of this chapter and encounter that potentially problematic word 'God', understand that it is being used in this sense: it is the energy that underpins and connects everything in the universe and, perhaps somewhat surprisingly, it is you.

GNOSTICISM: CUT OUT THE MIDDLE MAN

In one sense, Gnosticism refers to a collection of religious beliefs that developed in the first century among Christians and Jews, and were deemed heretical by the established church. As a result of this, many gnostic texts were destroyed. Others were carefully hidden.

However, they became significantly less obscure in the second half of the twentieth century after a collection of Gnostic texts was discovered near the Egyptian town of Nag Hammadi in 1945. These texts included extracts from the Gospel of Thomas, and the Gospel of Philip – versions of the life of Jesus that were excluded from the official Christian canon.

The first time a partial English translation of the texts appeared was in 1956 in the *Jung Codex* – thus named because the original had been acquired by the Carl Gustav Jung Institute in Zurich as a birthday present for Jung himself. Why did these texts make the perfect birthday present for Jung? Because Jung had long been fascinated by Gnosticism, and the core ideas expressed in Gnosticism in the first century closely echo the ideas that Jung developed in his work.

But why were these texts hidden in the first place? Why were they so dangerous to the established church? Because in another sense, Gnosticism is the fundamental belief that we do not need a church – or an intermediary like a priest – to guide us to a relationship with God (or, if you prefer, an understanding of our true self). Instead, we can cut out the middle man and have a direct relationship with God ourselves.

Gnosticism takes an idea that is mentioned in the canonical texts and expands on it. In the Gospel of Luke, we read 'The kingdom of God is within'. In Corinthians, Paul says, 'Know ye not that you are the temple of God and that the Spirit of God dwelleth in you?' The Gnostic gospels bring this idea to the forefront of Jesus's message. In the Gospel of Thomas, Jesus says, 'If your leaders say to you, "Look, the [Father's] kingdom is in the sky," then the birds of the sky will precede you. If they say to you, "It is in the sea," then the fish will precede you. Rather, the [Father's] kingdom is within you and it is outside you.'

The Gnostic Gospels also make it clear that Heaven and Hell are not places in the future, but states of mind that one can inhabit in the present. In the Gnostic view, it isn't sin that leads you to Hell, it is ignorance of who you truly are. As long as you don't know who you are, you will be in Hell right here and now.

The Gnostic message appears to be that Christ (and other prophets) did not bring a secret or a set of answers, but rather encouraged us to begin a process of enquiry ourselves. The way out of 'Hell' is a deep investigation of the self. The Gospel of Thomas says:

> If you bring forth what is within you, what you bring forth will save you. If you do not bring forth what is within you, what you do not bring forth will destroy you.

Jung would completely agree.

KABBALAH: A QUESTION OF BALANCE

The works of Dion Fortune, whose *Psychic Self-Defense* was one of Bowie's most prized books in Los Angeles, offer a relatively accessible and common-sense overview of magic and the Kabbalah (although not all her book titles are quite as snappy as *Psychic Self-Defense*). In *The Training and Work of the Initiate*, she writes, 'There are two paths to the innermost: the way of the mystic, which is the way of devotion and meditation, a solitary and subjective path; and the way of the occultist, which is the way of the intellect, of concentration and of the trained will… there is a path for each.'

It is fair to say that when you first approach the Kabbalah – the thousands of texts that comprise the more esoteric tradition of Jewish study – you will find that it focuses on what Fortune calls the occultist approach. ('Occult', by the way, is not a negative or pejorative term, even though a diet of horror films might have led you to believe otherwise.) Judaism prizes study and intellectual effort above virtually everything else, and the Kabbalah includes endless debate and discourse. The Kabbalah is open to interpretation because the Kabbalah *is* interpretation.

It also involves incredibly complex systems like the Tree of Life. This looks like a particularly intriguing board game. You can see Bowie sketching it in a photo that appeared on the 1991 CD reissue (and subsequent editions) of *Station to Station*. In the photo we can see that Bowie has drawn a clearly delineated Tree of Life on the floor, and sketched a rougher version on the wall behind him – where he has added a question mark. He is also scribbling and sketching in a notebook.

Forty years later – on the last occasion we ever see Bowie, in the video to his self-epitaph single 'Lazarus' – he is scribbling again in a notebook, wearing the same costume. Bowie didn't take decisions like that lightly. That his final communication contains an overt reference to the Kabbalah shows this was more than a fad for him.

The Tree of Life consists of ten sephirot, each of which represents one of the ways human beings can glimpse or understand Ein Sof. At its simplest, the Tree of Life is a lesson in the importance of balance: the left-hand side of the grid is Yin to the right-hand side's Yang. At its most complex, the Tree of Life is an intricate system of Russian dolls. Each sephirah (the singular form) contains all the other sephirot, and each operates in four separate worlds. Really, if such a thing could be drawn, the Tree of Life could accurately be represented as a ten-part Yin and Yang symbol, with each sephirah contained within *and* containing *and* equal to each other one. Times four.

Bowie cannot possibly have spent any time at all gazing on the Tree of Life without being consistently reminded that his life was hopelessly out of balance, consistently urged to find his way towards greater harmony, and consistently told that he *was* worth the effort.

MAGIC: IT'S JUST LIKE BILLIARDS, REALLY

'There is a single main definition of the object of all magic ritual. It is the uniting of the Microcosm with the Macrocosm. The Supreme and complete ritual is therefore the invocation of the Holy Guardian Angel; or, in the language of mysticism, Union with God.'

These are the words of Aleister Crowley, once called the wickedest man in the world. He doesn't sound very wicked, does he? This is one of the paradoxes within magic. From the outside, it looks intimidating, scary, threatening and potentially evil. When you start to read about it, however, it sounds reassuringly similar to the wisdom traditions that would more routinely be called philosophies or religions.

Of course, there have been individuals and groups who have deliberately created an air of mystery around the subject, and those who have tried to use magical powers for evil ends, but the core ideas are both benign and familiar.

The language of magic is different (and can be intimidating), but Crowley's message echoes Rabbi Moshe Cordovero's words: the microcosm (you) and the macrocosm (the divine, the universe) are fundamentally the same, and the aim of magic ritual is to reveal that connection.

This is Crowley, again: 'there is no distinction between magic and meditation, except of the most arbitrary and accidental kind.' So why do they seem so different?

This brings us back to Dion Fortune's distinction between the occultist and the mystic. In the mystic approach, one meditates – seeking direct connection with the divine (or, as we might prefer to phrase it, a better understanding of the true self). In the ritualistic, ceremonial or occultist approach, one follows prescribed and formal practices in the physical world.

However, magic follows a clear principle 'as above, so below', meaning the rituals that magicians carry out in the physical world are designed to have a direct effect in the mental plane. So genuine magicians, rather than hucksters, will understand that their rituals are meant to be physical representations of something that is actually happening psychologically. The real demons aren't in the swimming pool; they are in your mind.

The magician summoning and casting out an evil spirit is doing the same work as the Jungian therapist asking you to lie back on their couch and tell them about your dreams.

As Crowley put it, 'the spirit is merely a recalcitrant part of one's own organism. To evoke him is therefore to become conscious of some part of one's own character; to command and constrain him, is to bring that part into subjection. This is best understood by the analogy of teaching oneself some mental-physical accomplishment (e.g. billiards), by persistent and patient study and practice, which often involves considerable pain as well as trouble.'

Pausing only to savour the fact that when the wickedest man in the world is looking for an analogy for the magician's mighty battle against demons, the idea that first pops into his head is billiards, we will move on. And speaking of 'patient study and practice which often involves considerable pain as well as trouble' leads us quite neatly to alchemy.

ALCHEMY: FIRST TAME YOUR DRAGON

Alchemy is supposedly the art or science of turning base metal into gold. But an ancient alchemical tract states clearly: 'our gold is not the gold of the vulgar'. Some take this to mean that alchemists create a particularly pure form of the metal. Others take it to be a clear signal that alchemists are not interested in metal at all, but are fashioning a spiritual gold.

Alchemists employ an acronym VITRIOLUM, which represents the Latin expression '*Visita Interiora Terrae Rectificando Invenies Occultum Lapidem Veram Medicinam*', meaning 'Visit the interior of the Earth, and by rectifying you will find the hidden stone which is the true medicine'. In alchemy, as in mythology, the journey to the centre of the Earth represents a journey into your inner being, searching for your higher self. This journey into the interior – into the bowels of the Earth, into the underworld – inevitably means an encounter with demons and dragons, as does our journey into the deeper parts of our self. To find our way through our dark night of the soul, mythology suggests that we have to fight those demons and dragons but, as we will discover in Chapter 7, it might be more effective to befriend our demons and tame our dragons.

That word 'rectify', meaning to put right, is taken to mean that you reinstate your true nature. It's the alchemical equivalent of the Jungian process of individuation. The demons and dragons represent your shadow, which must be integrated into the self.

Alchemical texts refer to the process of turning metal into gold as 'the great work' and – echoing Socrates' dictum that 'the unexamined life is not worth living' – they suggest those who do not take up the great work are rather wasting their lives.

They also stress, however, that the great work is immensely challenging. One of the key stages of the alchemical process is '*solve et coagula*' – dissolve and coagulate. The phrase cannot help but remind us of the extraordinary transition of caterpillars into butterflies. When, as children, we first find out that caterpillars turn into butterflies, we imagine that a caterpillar steps into a chrysalis, grows a pair of wings and re-emerges. Job done. In fact, what happens within the chrysalis is an extraordinary and radical transformation in which the caterpillar effectively digests itself, dissolving completely except for a small group of cells, known as imaginal cells, which carry the blueprint for the creature who will eventually emerge.

Metamorphosis involves destruction as well as creation.

OUT OF THE ABYSS

If we grew up in the Western world, even if we are not remotely religious, we cannot help but be affected by the fundamental idea at the heart of the Abrahamic religions that there is something wrong with us, that we are fallen, that we have sinned, that we need to be saved. If and when we encounter Eastern religions, we are surprised to find a very different attitude: not only is there nothing wrong with us, but there is something very *right* with us – and we merely have to see through the illusions of our day-to-day existence to uncover this goodness.

Perhaps more surprisingly, when we look at the Western esoteric traditions, which include the less mainstream versions of Christianity and Judaism, we find a message that – instead of echoing the conventional Western religions – in fact echoes the message of the Eastern religions. Once again, the fundamental lesson is: there's nothing wrong with you. You do not need to be saved. You do not need to be fixed. You just need to realize who you are.

Within this more compassionate framework, we can summarize the lessons that Bowie may have learned – and that we can learn – from the esoteric teachings discussed in this chapter under the following four headings.

You're not on your own in this world. You are this world.

When we are in the middle of a dark night of the soul, we may feel we do not belong in this world. The lesson of Gnosticism and the Kabbalah is that not only do you belong in this world, but you are intimately connected to everyone and everything else. If we take this as our starting point – perhaps just intellectually to begin with if we don't *feel* it immediately – it has the potential to change how we view almost every aspect of our life.

You're not going to Hell after you die, but you might be there right now.

Again, even those without a religious bone in their body may still have this residual idea that we will be judged and quite possibly punished in some later life. The esoteric traditions tell us something very different.

You do not need to be saved because you have 'original sin'; you do not need to be fixed because you are wrong. You merely need to be led out of your confusion. It is simply ignorance of who you are that leaves you in a state of mind that could be described as Hell.

In fact, it's not quite true to say you need to be *led* out. You're going to have to find your own way out. The esoteric traditions, like the Eastern religions, simply point you in the right direction.

The demons aren't outside you. They're in your mind.

OK, so how do you get rid of this confusion? How do you see through the illusions? How do you find out who you really are? By journeying to the centre of the Earth, and confronting the demons and dragons that you find there. By looking further inside yourself, uncovering all the hidden aspects of your personality and successfully integrating them to reveal your true self.

(The word 'esoteric', by the way, doesn't mean, as you might imagine, 'difficult to understand' or 'obscure' or 'known by the few'. It means 'further in'. Esoteric wisdom simply points you inwards.)

When we're dealing in mythological metaphors, we are instructed to fight our demons. But it would be wrong – and unhelpful – to take this metaphor completely literally when we work on the psychological or spiritual level. When we look inside ourselves to find our own demons, our task is not to defeat them but to befriend them. In fact, trying hard to defeat your demons may be what has caused much of the misery in your life. The constant battle to subjugate parts of your personality can be both utterly exhausting and thoroughly demoralizing. Forming a better relationship with them is an urgent priority.

The 'great work' is hard work; but it's still your best option.

Confronting demons – whether we're going to fight them or somehow try to befriend them – sounds like a daunting task. It certainly is. But the alternative is to stay in crisis, to stay locked in a way of living that isn't working for you. Once you've started on the journey (and if you're reading this book, you probably have) it's better to finish it.

THE NEXT THREE RUNGS ON THE LADDER

As you begin your ascent from the bowels of the Earth, as you slowly climb out of the abyss, what are the next steps you have to take?

First, any dark night of the soul will almost certainly have made you question the way you have lived, and your purpose in life. So the first task is to clarify a sense of purpose and meaning that are consistent with (and will help you to define) the person you are now becoming. You can use the exercises that follow in the *Your Path* section to do this.

Second, we've talked about encountering demons and befriending them. Chapter 7 will clarify exactly what this means, and the exercises in the *Your Path* section of that chapter will show you exactly how to do it.

Third, we've also talked a lot about self, and about our 'true self'. Chapter 8 will explain in more detail what this means. At that point, we will return to Buddhism and explore the Buddhist concept of 'no self', but we will also introduce Frederick Nietzsche, a philosopher who – while being highly controversial – was clearly a very profound influence on Bowie's thinking.

YOUR PATH

At difficult times we might feel that life is directionless. It's important to reconnect with our purpose and to find meaning. The exercises in this section will help surface thoughts and feelings that can point you towards renewed purpose and meaning.

Remember the three questions from Bowie's teacher, Chime Rinpoche?

> Who are you?
>
> Where are you?
>
> Where are you going?

In this chapter we have concerned ourselves with those times in life when the answer to the question 'Where are you' is likely to be 'somewhere I don't like very much' or 'somewhere I don't want to be any more'. You need to quickly get some focus on where you are going. The exercises in this section will help generate thoughts and ideas that can lead you towards a direction of travel.

As you work through the exercises, allow that your answers might come in terms of a grand final destination for your journey or they might come in terms of simply knowing what the next step may be. Both are helpful. Both are valid.

Review: Who am I if…

Before you begin the new exercises in this section, take a moment to review your answers to the 'Who am I if…' questions at the end of each of the *Your Path* sections of the previous chapters. As a handy reminder, they are:

- Who am I if I don't judge?
- Who would I be without my childhood needs?
- Who would I be without my defences?
- Who am I if I am not the centre of the universe?
- Who am I if I am not my thoughts?

If you have answers to these questions, allow them to inform the work you do in the following exercises. If you do not yet have answers to these questions, allow the following exercises to help you review them.

Exercise: The past perspective

A recurring theme in the philosophies covered in this book is that we have a true understanding of ourselves and the world when we are young children, but that we lose this accurate picture of reality as we grow older, becoming immersed in the world of thought and confused by the materialist world around us.

In this light, spend some time thinking about the following question: 'What did you used to love that you have given up?'

Name as many things as you can think of (from any period of your life; you don't have to go all the way back to childhood) and include things that you gave up for very sensible, age-appropriate or life-stage-appropriate reasons. We are not necessarily looking for things you should start doing again now (although in some cases that might be an idea).

When you've put together a reasonable list, examine each item and ask yourself: 'What did I love about it?' Try to come up with a very clear answer that illuminates either a positive feeling that it gave you, a need of yours that it fulfilled, or some other clear benefit.

Then ask yourself what you have in your life now that gives you the same positive feeling, fulfils the same need or gives you the same clear benefit. If the answer is 'nothing', ask yourself if this is OK or if this is a gap that you would like to be filled. If so, how could you achieve that?

Exercise: The future perspective

Imagine your best possible future self.

Now imagine that this best possible future version of yourself is nearing the end of his or her life but is completely content. It has been a deeply satisfying life. Describe this life and outline why it was satisfying.

Now imagine that this best possible future self time-travels back to spend some time with you. What advice would he or she give you? Would you be able to hear it and act on it?

What questions would you like to ask your best possible future self?

Exercise: The present-day perspective

Every day for a week, at the end of the day, finish the following three sentences:

> Today, I most felt a sense of purpose when…
>
> Today, the most meaningful thing I did/said/was involved in was…
>
> Today, the most meaningful thing I observed someone else doing/saying was…

Write down why you felt the sense of purpose and why the event was meaningful.

Reflect on how you have chosen to define 'purpose' and 'meaning'.

Exercise: The atoms who think they are you

The Kabbalist sage Rabbi Moshe Cordovero said: 'All existence is God'. The physicist Frank Close, wrote:

> We are made of atoms. With each breath you inhale a million, billion, billion atoms of oxygen, which gives some

> idea of how small each one is. All of them, together with the carbon atoms in your skin, and indeed everything else on Earth, were cooked in a star some 5 billion years ago. So you are made of stuff that is as old as the planet, one-third as old as the universe… but this is the first time that those atoms have been gathered together such that they think that they are you.

I think those two quotations say very similar things. You may disagree. Take whichever idea you prefer: 'I am God,' or: 'I am made of stars,' and reflect on how this view of yourself might change things.

> How might it change how you see yourself?
>
> How might it change how you see others?
>
> How might it change your view of why you are here?

Your path: Going forward

1. Continue your regular meditation. From time to time introduce the following mantra to your meditation.

   Begin a simple breathing meditation.

   After a few minutes, when you are settled into the rhythm of the in breath and the out breath, gently lengthen and deepen each breath, and add a short pause, holding your breath between the in breath and the out breath for a few seconds. (Do not hold your breath for longer than is completely comfortable.)

Then begin to say this simple mantra to yourself (inside your head). As you breathe in, say to yourself, 'nowhere to go'. As you hold your breath, say to yourself, 'nothing to do'. As you breathe out – a long, slow out breath – say to yourself, 'no one to be'.

Repeat for several minutes.

2. If you had all the money you needed, if you no longer had to go to work, if – in fact – there was nothing that you actually *had* to do… what would you do? What would you do today? What would you do with the rest of your life? Try to answer this question in the broadest possible sense then carry the question with you for a while, answering it regularly and seeing if your answer changes.

3. Spend some time with this thought from the American mythologist Joseph Campbell: 'Life has no meaning. Each of us has meaning and we bring it to life. It is a waste to be asking the question when you are the answer.' Do you think this is true? And if you think it is true, does the idea that you are the answer thrill you or intimidate you?

4. For a week, begin every day with these two simple intentions:

   I will find meaning in everything I do today.

I will do everything I do today with purpose.

At the end of the day, reflect on how you were (or were not) able to find meaning, and how you were (or were not) able to act with purpose. Do not judge yourself harshly for the times when you weren't able to act with purpose or find meaning; rather, celebrate each moment when you do so.

IF YOU NEED HELP, ASK FOR IT

The purpose of this book is to help you grow as a person, to help you discover your true nature. Within those terms, the purpose of this chapter is to reinforce the fact that this growth can occur – and may, in fact, be accelerated – during our darkest moments. We are proceeding on the basis that difficult times (like those experienced by Bowie in 1975) can be harnessed for our benefit.

This is true. However, it won't always be true for everyone. While the exercises in this chapter and throughout the book can be extremely beneficial when working through such dark times, it would be foolish to suggest that everyone will always be able (as Bowie was) to rebuild a fractured personality without professional help.

If you find that the ideas in this book are not enough, if you feel stuck, if you feel you cannot find a way through, then please consider talking to your doctor and exploring the professional help that is available.

Similarly, some people may – in such difficult transitional periods – experience suicidal thoughts or feelings. To a certain extent, thoughts about death are natural at times like this because, in a sense, a part of you is dying. You are replacing a false sense of yourself with a more real sense of yourself. Some people will find it possible to frame occasional thoughts about death in this way, to stay with them and work through them. (We'll look at exactly how to do this in Chapter 7. If you don't want to wait, skip ahead to page 228 now.)

However, just because some people can do a lot of this work on their own, it doesn't mean that everyone should do so without support. If occasional suicidal thoughts and feelings become more frequent, if they will not leave you, or if they start to move beyond thoughts and feelings into actually planning how you might kill yourself then, once again, please seek professional help.

CHAPTER 7: SHADOW

The life lesson: Make friends with your shadow side

You can escape everything except yourself.

(Julian Priest, David Bowie's character in TV series The Hunger*)*

Every treasure is guarded by dragons. That's how you can tell it's valuable.

(Saul Bellow, Herzog*)*

Perhaps the only pain that can be avoided is the pain that comes from trying to avoid pain.

(R. D. Laing)

BOWIE'S PATH

In 1976 Bowie relocated to Berlin, taking with him his friend (and fellow addict) Iggy Pop. They planned to support each other in reducing their drug dependency, while – in both his life and his songwriting – Bowie began to examine who he really was.

You may be aware that in some cultures, at some points in history, left-handed people were considered unlucky, or even evil. You may have assumed this was many centuries ago, back when people still ducked women into ponds to see if they were witches.

In fact, the idea was still vividly alive in 1950s Britain, and the young David Jones's classmates delighted in shouting 'Devil!' as he walked by simply because he wrote with his left hand. As well as inviting ridicule – and sometimes bullying – from his classmates, his left-handedness invited physical abuse from his teachers, who would smack his left hand if he tried to write with it.

This was not an uncommon experience at the time, and it illustrates the kind of cultural pressure that can encourage an individual to bury or subsume a completely natural part of themselves, feeling that it is unwanted or bad (or even evil). These are the kinds of moments that can lead to the development of what Jung termed the shadow – an unconscious repository of any aspects of our personality that we learn are unacceptable.

The moments in our childhood that build the shadow can be vivid and obvious, like the smacking of a young boy's hand when they use the 'wrong' hand to write with. They can also be insidious and virtually invisible, like the cold atmosphere of Bowie's childhood home. One would normally say the shadow is the place where an individual buries unwanted emotions. In the case of Bowie, however, he learned at a very young age that *all* emotions were unwanted and, based on the descriptions of people who met him in the late 1960s and early 1970s, it does not seem too much of an exaggeration to suggest that he did indeed bury almost his entire emotional life in his unconscious shadow, leaving on the conscious level a cold, calculating, emotion-free personality. Bowie referred to himself at this time as 'a robot'.

Bowie was well aware of Jung's concept of individuation and understood that this process of self-realization would involve bringing the contents of his shadow back into conscious awareness, while at the same time discarding the personas that he had been wearing in public. He knew that integrating elements of his shadow was a path to discovering his true self, but he was also aware that this reintegration of the shadow would take courage, strength and time.

Bowie was fascinated by the concept of the shadow. He wrote about it repeatedly throughout his career, starting with 1967's 'Shadow Man', continuing through 'The Man Who Sold The World' and 'The Width of a Circle', and then returned to the subject in several of his Berlin songs, including 'Breaking Glass' and 'Beauty and the Beast'. He engaged with the concept again on his *Scary Monsters* album, and shadow characters appear in videos from songs on his final two albums.

Bowie clearly knew his shadow was there and that it was important. He also knew that Jung had warned against the dangers of ignoring it:

> A man who has not passed through the inferno of his passions has never overcome them. They may dwell in the house next door, and at any moment a flame may dart out and set fire to his own house. Whenever we give up, leave behind, and forget too much, there is always the danger that the things we have neglected will return with added force.

In this passage from *Memories Dreams Reflections*, Jung seems to portray us as innocent bystanders, suddenly sabotaged by our shadows. But once we know there is a shadow, and once we know that leaving it unexamined in remote, unconscious darkness can lead to all sorts of problems – anxiety, phobias, depression, addiction – then if we don't at least *consider* doing the work of individuation, we are effectively self-sabotaging. As Jung also said: 'a man who is possessed by his Shadow is always standing in his own light and falling into his own traps'.

In 'Word on a Wing', Bowie's 'prayer' on the *Station to Station* album, he shares his understanding that he has indeed been standing in his own light, and defiantly states his intention to never do it again.

WHY BERLIN? WHY IGGY?

Having committed to stripping away his personas and confronting his shadow, Bowie decided that the best place to do this would be Berlin, and the best possible companion for this journey into himself would be Iggy Pop.

These are, on the surface, two strange decisions. Berlin was, at that time, the heroin capital of the world (a title it arguably shared with Amsterdam but, whereas heroin had a street value of $130 a gram in the Dutch capital, in Berlin you could find it at half that price), and Iggy Pop was a heroin addict trying to clean up.

Conventional wisdom would suggest Berlin would not be the right place to go, and Pop would not be the right person to go with. So why did Bowie make these decisions?

Bowie was always deeply affected by his environment. He always drew parallels between his inner world and the world around him. In moving to Berlin, Bowie was moving to a city that reflected his inner state, a city whose fundamental problem mirrored *his* fundamental problem.

Bowie was a man divided: on one side was his conscious self; on the other side was his unconscious shadow. And he knew he desperately needed to break down the wall between them and integrate both sides.

Berlin was a city divided: on one side was the West; on the other side was the grim, Communist East. And in the city was a population that desperately wanted to break down the wall that divided it and reunite friends and families who had been kept apart by the forbidding barrier.

Bowie didn't just move to a city that was cut in half by a wall; he booked into a studio that was located within sight of that wall and overlooked by an East German gun turret. The East German guards literally looked into the studio where Bowie was recording and he looked out onto the barbed wire. He was continually reminded of the external barrier, even as he worked to break down his internal barrier.

If Berlin was the perfect environment for the work Bowie needed to do, why was Iggy the perfect companion? Bowie knew part of this individuation process would involve letting go of the personas he had created, and the core persona on which the rest were built was Ziggy Stardust. The similarity between the names Iggy and Ziggy is not a coincidence. When Bowie toured the US in 1971 and first saw Iggy Pop perform live, he hurriedly scribbled down notes of a new character that could form the basis of the songs on his next album. Ziggy *was* Iggy.

Admittedly, Ziggy Stardust also has roots in other people (including the briefly successful British rock-and-roll star Vince Taylor, whose sharp career decline inspired the storyline of the *Ziggy Stardust* album, and the Legendary Stardust Cowboy, who gave Ziggy his surname). Yet there is no doubt it was Iggy's famously extreme live performances that truly entranced Bowie, forming the foundation of the character that would propel him to fame.

This is why Iggy was the perfect companion in Berlin. Bowie could discard his rock-and-roll star persona because, with Pop by his side, he didn't need it any more. He didn't need to play at being like Iggy Pop when Iggy Pop could do that for him. If he wanted to hide behind an Iggy Pop persona, he could simply hide behind Iggy Pop (as indeed he did, when he toured as the keyboard player in Iggy's band for several weeks during 1977).

There were, of course, many other aspects to their relationship, including genuine friendship and empathetic creative collaboration, but crucially during this particular period – with Iggy close at hand and Bowie's internal world physically drawn out in the landscape of Berlin around him – Bowie found that, 'for the first time, the tension was outside me rather than within me'.

A SHORT, SHARP SHOCK

It was common during the 1970s for people of an earlier generation seeing rock stars like David Bowie or the punks that followed him – with their outlandish costumes and outrageous behaviour – to say that what they needed was 'a short, sharp shock'. The older generation, who had lived through a war, would routinely suggest this could best be provided by national service in the military.

At the end of 1976, Bowie decided to deliver a short, sharp shock to himself by adopting a lifestyle that was severely limited compared to his time in LA. Pictures of him at the time show the man who had been a fashion icon and trendsetter for the past five years wearing jeans and a lumberjack shirt. He bought himself a bike – not a fancy bike, a simple three-speed Raleigh bike – and he cycled from his apartment at Hauptstrasse 155 to the studio. When he wasn't on his bike, he was on public transport. He went shopping for his own groceries. And, like any normal person, he was annoyed when his flatmate (Iggy) ate them.

When the pair returned to the flat in the evening, their big treat was to sit and watch the latest episode of *Starsky & Hutch*, just like regular folks. 'Berlin was my clinic,' said Bowie later. 'It brought me back in touch with people.'

Part of his new regime was to reduce his reliance on drugs. Iggy eloquently described the Berlin scene as 'an artsy-craftsy weekend drug culture', as opposed to the 24/7 supply on the west coast of America. They would still indulge but not relentlessly. Bowie ended his cocaine use. They both drank but stayed sober during working hours. Physically during this period Bowie's health improved and he put on weight.

He was well aware that his stripped-back lifestyle was still a very privileged one compared to some others. Although he was buying his own groceries, he was buying them at KaDeWe – a distinctly upmarket department store. He lived close by the area in Berlin occupied by poor Turkish immigrants, and dwelled on both the economic hardship and racial discrimination they suffered. He said his song 'Heroes', written in Berlin, was about the daily struggle of the Turkish immigrants, 'facing that kind of reality and standing up to it', and about just getting on with things 'from the very simple pleasure of remaining alive'. Even when artists claim to not be writing about themselves, of course they really are, and this account of the economic and racial pressures Turkish immigrants faced is also a song about the psychological pressure Bowie was experiencing as he confronted his shadow. 'I stripped myself down,' he said, 'and took myself apart layer by layer.'

THE LIFE LESSON: MAKE FRIENDS WITH YOUR SHADOW SIDE

To grow as a person, we need to integrate all aspects of our personality, including the hidden – previously rejected – parts of ourselves that Jung referred to as the shadow. It's not an easy process – in part because most of us have never been taught how to manage difficult and uncomfortable emotions. But we can learn to do this.

Although it wasn't until the twentieth century that Carl Jung formalized the idea of individuation and the concept of integrating the shadow, the basic idea had been known for centuries on some level. This is clear because it features again and again in fiction. We can see it in the Victorian novel, *The Strange Case of Dr Jekyll and Mr Hyde* by Robert Louis Stevenson, in which the respectable Dr Jekyll tries to cordon off all the unwanted parts of his personality into his alter ego, Mr Hyde. His inability to encompass all sides of his personality in one integrated self has disastrous, murderous consequences. We see a similar theme explored in the many folktales of werewolves, which date back at least 2000 years, and more recently in the Marvel Comics universe, where the mild-mannered Dr Bruce Banner and his city-smashing counterpart, the Incredible Hulk, are a modern version of Jekyll and Hyde.

We also see the individuation process and the integration of the shadow played out repeatedly in children's stories. Every princess who kisses a frog, who then turns into a prince, is travelling along the journey of individuation – doing something that at first seems counterintuitive, distasteful or even frightening in order to reap a great reward. *Beauty and the Beast* tells a similar story: that if we can learn to stay with what we initially find frightening, we will receive a great benefit.

Thanks to the comparative studies of Joseph Campbell, we know that similar stories can be found in cultures around the world: the hero who journeys into the underworld or the diver who plunges in the murky sea may have to fight dragons or monsters to get the treasure they seek or to finish their quest, but eventually they return to the surface, or surface world, triumphant and transformed. The monsters are the shadow; the acquisition of the treasure symbolizes the realization of the true self.

We all, if we accept the challenging work of individuation, need to embark on our own hero's journey. Campbell says this:

> It is by going down into the abyss that we recover the treasures of life. Where you stumble, there lies your treasure. The very cave you're afraid to enter turns out to be the source of what you're looking for. The damned thing in the cave that was so dreaded has become the center.

A CAVE FULL OF DEMONS

Speaking of caves, the Buddhist story that best illustrates this theme is that of Milarepa's Cave.

Milarepa has been out gathering firewood. When he returns to his cave, he finds it is inhabited by demons – fierce, snarling demons trashing his cave and roaring in rage. Milarepa is understandably scared and doesn't know how to deal with the situation. His first thought is that he has to get rid of the demons, and his first action is to try to chase them out of the cave. However, the demons merely laugh at him and refuse to leave.

Then Milarepa – as a good Buddhist student – thinks: 'Well, I've received a lot of teachings about right thinking and right action. I could use these. I could use my intellectual study to defeat these demons,' and he begins to teach them the Dharma, to talk them through everything that he's learned about self and non-self, the nature of impermanence, the concept of emptiness. The demons do not move. They do not leave.

Milarepa shrugs his shoulders and realizes he cannot actually get rid of the demons. 'OK,' he says, 'fair enough. It looks like you're going to be here for a while. We're just going to have to find a way to live together. You know, if you've got something you want to say to me, say it. If there's something you want to do, do it. If you want to trash the place, trash the place. I really can't stop you. We'll just somehow find a way of coexisting here.'

And in that moment, all the demons disappear… except one. The largest, fiercest, most frightening demon remains. Milarepa sighs and shrugs and walks over to the demon. Then he does something extraordinary: he places his head in the demon's mouth. 'If you want to eat me,' he says, 'eat me.' And in this moment, when Milarepa has completely surrendered to him, the largest, fiercest demon bows and leaves the cave.

In this story we encounter the twist mentioned in the previous chapter. That is, whereas most myths and stories in Western culture suggest our task when we encounter demons is to defeat them, Milarepa's story teaches us something very different: that the way to deal with demons is to accept them. His final strategy is not to try to fix the problem, but to stay with it – to surrender to reality. And in this way, he finds freedom.

Is putting your head in a demon's mouth a sensible thing to do? On the surface, it doesn't seem as though it is. So let's explore each stage of Milarepa's reactions to the demons to see what the story tells us.

The first stage is simply awareness. When Milarepa returns to the cave, he is aware of the demons. That doesn't sound too difficult. If you walked into a cave and it was full of demons you would probably notice them too. But within the metaphor, it's important that Milarepa can actually see the demons. They are aspects of Milarepa's personality that he has previously pushed down, suppressed or ignored. On this occasion, he's finally aware of them. To switch from Buddhist analogy to Jungian terminology, this is the moment when he realizes that he has a shadow.

Stage two is the instinctive and entirely understandable reaction to try and chase the demons away. When Milarepa realizes just how scary his shadow is, he tries to push it away. He tries to make the demons leave but, unsurprisingly, he is unsuccessful.

Stage three is interesting. It's a completely intellectual response. He decides to use his learnings, the Buddha's teachings, to deal with the demons. But a purely intellectual response – as Buddha would tell you, as Jung would tell you – is not enough. Knowing things (knowing, for example, that demons are not real, that they are merely aspects of your own personality) is not enough. As anyone who has been in therapy knows, the intellectual bit – the insight, the 'aha' moment – is just the beginning.

What is needed is an emotional response. We need to meet our edge and soften. Our response must be one of complete acceptance of the demons and their nature – and this is Milarepa's next response. He says to the demons, 'OK, let's stay in the cave together.' It is a commitment to stay with difficult emotions, to stay with parts of his personality that previously he would have denied or suppressed. This is the key turning point. When we resist or push away, we make things worse. When we accept, the power of our demons lessens. The things we fear become less frightening.

At this point in Milarepa's story most of the demons leave. The most frightening demon remains. Milarepa has to summon all his courage and move beyond acceptance to complete and utter surrender. When he is able to do this, his final demon leaves.

Milarepa doesn't conquer his demons by fighting them. Indeed, he doesn't conquer them at all. He learns to stay with them, to coexist with them, to surrender to them. And in that way, they cease to be frightening demons at all. Milarepa's response points to the best way of integrating our shadow: by accepting what arises and then by staying with what arises. That will indeed, for a time, feel a bit like putting your head in the demon's mouth.

Milarepa says to the demon: 'Do your worst.'

We say to our emotions: 'I'm ready to feel you completely now.'

FEELING OUR FEELINGS

In order to meet our shadow, in order to befriend our demons, what we need is to be able to cope with the feelings that will arise when we explore our shadow side.

That is all we have to do. It is also a frightening task.

So many of us find it difficult to simply feel our feelings. Why is this? There are many reasons. The most glaringly obvious, however, is that we simply don't know how to do it. The vast majority of us have never been *taught* how to feel our feelings.

Have *you* ever been taught how to feel your feelings? It's extremely unlikely that you have. I have asked this question in many training sessions over the years and I've only ever had a handful of people say they had been taught how to feel their feelings. None, by the way, were taught this valuable skill by their parents or at school – the institution designed to prepare young people for life. The tiny percentage of people who had received instructions in how to feel their feelings had done so on previous mindfulness courses.

Not only do most of us not know how to feel our feelings, many of us don't even know that feeling our feelings is an option.

Many people think they have only two options when they experience a feeling that they consider difficult, uncomfortable or negative: they can bury it or push it away. They can use a variety of psychological defences (like the ones we discussed in Chapter 3) to bury their feelings, or they can 'take the feeling out' on someone else. If they're angry, they become angry *at* someone – shouting at whoever happens to be nearby. They are unaware of the third (and infinitely preferable) option of simply feeling the feeling – simply staying with it.

Another reason why people struggle to feel their feelings is that they don't know what they are. Many people have problems identifying what they are feeling or labelling the feelings as they arise. We tend to grow up with a very limited emotional vocabulary.

Another barrier is that many of us have difficulty understanding the difference between a thought and a feeling. This confusion is made worse by the way our language works. If I ask someone I'm coaching how they felt in a particular situation, they are quite likely to reply with a sentence that begins 'I felt that…' or 'I felt like…'

Confusingly, sentences that begin 'I feel that…' or 'I feel like…' will almost always describe thoughts not feelings. Similarly, sentences that begin 'I feel he…' or 'I feel you…' will likely be thoughts and judgements, not feelings.

On top of all these reasons why feeling our feelings can be difficult, there are two additional factors that make feeling the feelings we have buried in our shadow even more problematic. First, they have been buried there for a long time and therefore we are naturally wary of them. Second, we buried them there originally because we believed (on some level) that they were 'bad', that they were not meant to be felt. Both of these factors can lead us to question our ability to cope with these feelings if they surface now.

In fact, as we can see from the example of Bowie, many of the feelings we bury are not 'difficult' or 'problematic' or 'bad' at all. We've just been led to believe they are by those around us. Equally, however, some of us will have buried genuinely traumatic moments.

Whatever your situation, you should approach the work in the next section cautiously, beginning by processing milder feelings and only gradually increasing the intensity of the feelings you can manage. Do this gently and with kindness towards yourself. And consider seeking support from others if it feels appropriate.

YOUR PATH

Making friends with your shadow may release long-buried feelings. To help you cope with this – and to help you manage your emotional life in general – this section offers techniques that allow you to process 'difficult' feelings within a kind and loving framework.

In this section we are using the words 'feeling' and 'emotion' interchangeably. Technically, they are slightly different, but for our purposes it makes sense to treat them as essentially the same because, in normal speech, we use the two words to mean the same thing. Besides, although experts divide them into two separate things, they can't actually agree on what the difference is – so let's not get caught up in this confusing area. Also, there is a far more important distinction that I want you to keep in mind: the distinction between the two component parts of a feeling.

Our feelings contain two elements: a physical sensation in the body and an accompanying thought (or usually a succession of thoughts). In the work we do here, we will focus on the physical sensation and, mirroring our meditation work, we will let the thoughts go.

Exercise: Naming emotions

As we've noted above, one of the strongest barriers to truly feeling our feelings is not having a large enough emotional vocabulary, and thus not being able to discriminate between different feelings and label them appropriately.

As soon as we are able to correctly identify and name our feelings, we are better able to manage our emotional life. In many instances, simply being able to correctly identify and name what you are feeling will be enough to make a 'difficult' emotion much easier to handle.

Step one of this exercise is to simply think of as many feelings or emotions as you can and to write them all down. Don't read on until you've done this.

Now, step two. Take the word 'sad' or 'sadness' (I'm going to assume you wrote that down). Look through this list of feelings that are closely related to sadness. We could say that they are variations or subdivisions of sadness:

- anguished
- lonely
- miserable
- disappointed
- gloomy
- friendless
- discouraged

- ignored
- rejected
- empty
- troubled
- melancholy
- depressed
- weary.

We're not simply playing with a thesaurus here. These words are not the same as sadness; they all have their own specific meaning. If you can get to a stage where your emotional vocabulary is so rich that you can distinguish between many types of sadness, you will be even better able to manage your emotional life.

Step three is to go back to the other words you wrote down on your list and, for each one, come up with some variations – in the same way that the listed words above are variations on sadness.

When you run out, google 'a list of human emotions' or something similar for inspiration. The object of this exercise is not to test your current limits but to expand them.

Technique: How to name a feeling

Now that you have a vocabulary to describe your emotions, how should you use it?

Remember that when we discussed your relationship with your thoughts in Chapter 5, I encouraged you to talk about your thoughts in a very specific way – one that emphasizes that you are not your thoughts but that you are the observer of your thoughts. Similarly, you are not your feelings. You are the observer of your feelings.

Practise describing your feelings in this way, even though it initially sounds slightly silly. Rather than saying 'I am angry,' for example, say to yourself: 'I am currently observing a physical sensation in my body that I identify as anger.'

It's not what we would normally say. But that's the point. It happens to be a much more accurate way of describing what is going on. And it creates a sense of space around the feeling, which makes it easier for you to stay with a feeling that previously you might have found too uncomfortable.

HOW TO FEEL A FEELING, PART 1: THE R.E.A.L. MEDITATION

R.E.A.L. stands for Recognize, Experience, Accept, Love. It's a technique for handling 'difficult' emotions. (But really it's a way to feel *all* feelings.)

Human beings have evolved to think of some feelings or emotions as 'difficult' or 'unwanted'. When we're sad, for example, we sometimes think this is 'wrong' – that we should be happy – and that we should try to push feelings like that away. But pushing 'difficult' feelings away doesn't help. They just come back – usually stronger than before. Counterintuitively, embracing 'difficult' feelings makes them more manageable. So:

*We **Recognize** them.* We label them, give them a name. The simple fact of describing your feeling, giving it a name, reduces its power to upset or derail you. It recalibrates your relationship with the feeling.

*We **Experience** them.* We locate the feeling in our body. We quieten our busy minds, and focus solely on where the feeling is in our body.

*We **Accept** them.* We welcome them as we would welcome an old friend.

*We **Love** them.* We offer them our attention, our caring and our love.

Now, why on earth would I suggest you should love a part of yourself that, up to this point, you probably don't even like very much? In fact, you may actively *dis*like your sadness, your anger or your other 'negative' emotions.

Let's, for now, work with sadness.

Loving your sadness may not be what you instinctively want to do, but it is what your sadness needs from you. To make this easier to understand, let's externalize things. Let's imagine that, instead of your internal sadness, it's a child of yours or a dear friend who is sad.

If your child/friend is sad, do you love them less? No. Do you give them your time and attention? Yes. Do you say, 'Go away, leave me alone, I don't want to see you again until you're happy and everything's going well'? No, you don't. But many of us effectively say this to ourselves when we're sad, using any technique we can think of (alcohol is a favourite) to numb the feeling.

In this exercise, in this meditation, we see that our own sadness is the same as that of a sad child or sad friend. It is in need of our time and care and love. If we give it our time and care and love, it will evolve naturally and we will move through the emotion.

By giving our loving attention to our child or friend, we can help them to move through their sadness and come out the other side. We can do the same thing for ourselves.

This is a meditation to do when you have a 'difficult' or 'negative' feeling. Don't wait until you have an intense feeling to try it for the first time. Instead, you can practise by simply recalling an event that triggered a slightly 'negative' feeling. Practise with mild feelings; don't practise with trauma.

A note on the 'L' word

If you find it too difficult to say that you love your emotions or that you love yourself, it's OK to substitute the word 'like' for 'love' throughout this meditation. If you find even that difficult, you can initially substitute a thought like 'this is OK' or 'I'm OK.'

The meditation

Sit comfortably – relaxed but alert. And close your eyes.

Now, simply focus on the breath. Become aware of the rhythm of the in breath and the out breath.

You will be distracted by thoughts – that chattering voice we all have in our head – because all humans are. When thoughts arise, gently push them away, let them float away, and return your focus to your breath: in breath… out breath…

Now, focus on your feelings. What are you feeling right now?

(For the purposes of this exercise, we're going to use sadness. Obviously you will replace sadness with whatever you are actually feeling. If you want to practise staying with a 'difficult' emotion but you're feeling fine right now, at this point in the meditation recall a recent moment/incident when you felt the 'difficult' feeling. Recall it vividly; imagine you are back in that moment – see what you saw, hear what you heard – and the feeling will return.)

Now **recognize** and name the feeling. Don't say 'I'm sad' because that's not what's actually happening here. You are observing sadness in your body. So, say to yourself 'I can observe a physical sensation in my body that I identify as sadness.'

Now locate and **experience** exactly where it is in your body. Maybe the throat, chest, belly…

Now describe what it feels like: tight, heavy, sharp, dull, light, warm, cold? Describe it. Don't judge it ('my chest feels tight' not 'my chest feels horrible').

Now **accept it**. Welcome it: 'Hello, sadness, my old friend. I have made some time for you in my busy schedule. Let's spend some time together.'

If the feeling is unpleasant, try to stay with it. That's our practice. (But if it's too much, if it's overwhelming, simply return your focus to your breath. Or just open your eyes. Try the meditation again another time with a less intense feeling. If you practise with gentle feelings, you'll gradually be able to manage stronger ones.)

Next place your hand on your heart. Feel the pressure of your hand on your chest. Vary the pressure a bit, so you're really locked into that contact.

Now send yourself a message of **love**. Right into your heart. Let the 'sad you' know that you love him or her as much as you love the happy you. Your love for yourself is unconditional.

You have now done something extraordinary. Instead of pushing your 'difficult' feeling away, you have held your 'difficult' emotion in a place of love. What does that feel like?

Stay in this place where you can feel both the 'difficult' emotion and the love together for as long as you can.

Then – very slowly, very gently, in your own time – just move your focus back out of your body.

And as slowly and gently as you like, open your eyes.

HOW TO FEEL A FEELING, PART 2: THE 'TEA WITH MARA' PROCESS

We can't always meditate. But, using this process, we can take the elements of the REAL meditation and apply them even when we are sitting at our desk at work.

In Buddhist psychology, Mara is a demon – he is, if you like, Buddha's 'arch-enemy'.

But Mara is not the devil. Mara is part of Buddha. He represents the parts of us we would like to push away – the difficult or unwanted bits. Counterintuitively, Buddha taught that we should welcome these feelings.

In one version of the stories that are told about Buddha and Mara, Buddha invites Mara to join him for tea. When Buddha does this, he is not actually inviting a demon to tea. He's committing to staying with a 'difficult' feeling.

Our practice is: to commit to staying with a feeling for a few minutes. The tea symbolizes that we *choose* to do this, that we will do this kindly – with love for ourselves.

We practise with a mildly uncomfortable feeling, not with trauma.

The process

1. Make a mug of tea. If you don't like tea, this step is entirely optional, but a warm, comforting hot beverage can help the process along.

2. Identify the feeling. Name it.

3. Breathe. Let thoughts go.

4. Find the feeling in your body. Locate the physical sensation.

5. Commit to staying with it for an agreed period of time (such as while drinking your tea).

6. Do all of this kindly. With love.

7. When thoughts take over, breathe again and turn your attention back to your body.

Ideally you would find a quiet place and moment to do this, but you don't have to. It's perfectly possible to go through the 'tea with Mara' process at your desk at work or in a crowded cafe. No one else knows what you are doing.

Your path: Going forward

1. Continue the regular breathing meditation practice that you have established in earlier chapters.
2. Commit to pausing for a certain number of times every day to simply ask yourself: 'What am I feeling?' If this proves difficult, print out a list of human feelings or emotions. Stick it on the wall somewhere and look at it regularly to refresh your emotional vocabulary.
3. As you go through the day and notice emotions, ask yourself whether you are treating each emotion as a friend or a foe. Having in all probability spent years or decades regarding certain emotions as 'negative' or 'unwanted', it will take a while to readjust. So go out of your way to claim emotions as your friends. If they persist, find the time to go through the *Tea with Mara* or *REAL meditation* process with them.
4. We learned from Bowie's example that many aspects of ourselves that we consign to our shadow side are not in any way wrong or bad. Bearing this in mind, consider the question: 'If I integrate my shadow, who am I?'

CHAPTER 8: HEROES

The life lesson: Keep searching till you find your true self

I wanted to see what I was like, and what kind of things I wanted to express rather than the characters I created.

(David Bowie)

Ultimately, one has to return to zero. There's no reference point any more, just zero.

(Chögyam Trungpa Rinpoche, True Perception: The Path of Dharma Art*)*

Become who you are.

(Frederick Nietzsche's epigram on his graduate essay, quoting the Greek poet Pindar)

BOWIE'S PATH

The search for the self can be long and complicated, full of tangents and cul-de-sacs. Having found himself during the Berlin years, Bowie then spectacularly lost himself again in the 1980s – distracted by the spectacular success of *Let's Dance*. Ironically, it was his much-maligned Tin Machine project that refocused him on his journey of self-discovery.

The seventeenth-century philosopher Blaise Pascal famously wrote that 'all of humanity's problems stem from man's inability to sit quietly in a room alone.'

You cannot discover your true self unless you are prepared to spend some time sitting quietly alone, but many of us would rather do anything else. It isn't just Pascal's view that we struggle to spend time alone in a room with our thoughts; 350 years after he wrote that line, social psychologists at the University of Virginia in Charlottesville provided the scientific evidence to prove his point.

In their research study, participants were asked to sit in a sparsely furnished room for a period of fifteen minutes and just think, having put away all belongings such as laptops, phones, notebooks and pens. There were several different variations of the experiment. In one version, the participants were left alone for fifteen minutes, asked to do nothing except think, but were also told that they had one possible alternative to quiet self-reflection: if they wanted to they could push a button that would give them a painful electric shock.

This was, let's be clear, not a strange group of participants who enjoyed pain. All of them had stated in previous written tests that they would pay money to *avoid* being shocked with electricity. However, rather than just sit there quietly and think, 67 per cent of men and 25 per cent of women chose to inflict a painful electric shock upon themselves.

The extent to which we will go to avoid being alone with our thoughts is remarkable. It might be painful electric shocks. It might be years of cocaine addiction. It might be workaholism. It might be dressing up and playing a series of characters that we are slowly coming to despise.

After years of avoidance, the lyrics of 1977's *Low* give us David Bowie sitting in a room alone with his thoughts. Where once he had written songs about outrageous creatures, he now wrote about himself. Where once his canvas was outer space, his songs were now set in a room with the blinds drawn.

There aren't many lyrics on *Low*. Bowie doesn't have much to say. He hardly knows himself yet, so what *could* he say? He knows there are feelings lurking within, but he doesn't yet know what they all are. And this is about as much as we can glean from the fragmentary words on side one of the album.

Insightfully, Bowie referred to his inability to write many lyrics for the album not as writer's block but as a bottleneck. He wasn't empty of ideas. There was a lot that wanted to get out; it just couldn't get out yet. There are virtually no reference points.

The music doesn't sound like anything else. The lyrics offer the listener hardly anything to grasp hold of in terms of meaning. More than half the album is instrumental. Bowie has taken the advice of his one-time teacher and returned to zero. It's a return to zero in another sense too. Bowie referred to Berlin as his 'womb': a place to feel safe again; a place to be reborn; a place to reconnect.

When the music magazine *NME*, at the end of the millennium, named Bowie as the most influential artist of all time and asked him about his most influential albums, *Low* and *Heroes*, Bowie was not particularly concerned with discussing their extraordinary innovation or their widespread influence. He preferred to explain their role in his life, saying simply: 'There was a certain healing going on, spiritually and emotionally.'

Many fans consider them to be Bowie's best albums, and it can't be a coincidence that these are also the first albums on which the real Bowie starts to appear from beneath the masks – the first albums on which the listener feels genuinely connected, not simply to Bowie's creative brilliance but to his emotions. We can't always be sure what he's singing about, but we can tell he is sad.

While the mood of *Low* is sad, it is not depressed. When you confront your shadow, you may find there is sadness there, as Bowie does, but it is when you *avoid* your shadow that you can become depressed. Indeed, Bowie said that within the sadness of *Low*, he can hear real optimism:

> 'I can hear myself really struggling to get well.'

In writing his book *David Bowie: Fame Sound and Vision*, sociologist Nick Stevenson conducted many interviews with Bowie's fans, and wrote that, 'I was struck by how many people mentioned listening to *Low* as a way of helping them through depressive periods. The mournful music of *Low* gave voice to Bowie's own inner turmoil and also helps many of his listeners deal with their own.'

COMPASSION

During the early 1970s Bowie found it easy to write for other people but hard to write for himself. He could write a song for Mott the Hoople far more easily than he could write a song for David Bowie. This was one of his justifications for his continued use of characters. He could write a song for Ziggy Stardust or the Thin White Duke because he knew who they were much more clearly than he knew who David Bowie was.

He had no idea what David Bowie wanted to sing.

In 1976, writing the songs for *Low*, he began to find out. By the next year, writing the songs for *Heroes*, he had connected with himself more fully and could both write and sing the emotionally richer songs of that album, including the title track, which is both one of his most iconic vocal performances and also probably the song in his canon that emotionally connects with more people than any other. The robot had found his heart.

He had reconnected with himself by reconnecting with other people. Every day in Berlin he committed to acting more 'normally', to being less insulated. He felt a real sense of achievement as he learned to simply talk to people again.

Having come out from his seclusion to interact with the rest of the world, Bowie found that he now cared about it. In an interview promoting the album, he told Allan Jones of *Melody Maker*, '*Heroes* is I hope compassionate, compassionate for people and the silly desperate situations they've gotten themselves into – that we've all got ourselves into.'

On another occasion he suggested that the message of the title track was on one level 'We can get out of this,' and on another, more personal level, 'I'll be OK.'

DISTRACTION

Nick Stevenson concludes simply that *Heroe*s articulates 'the possibility of reconstructing the self'. That is precisely our task.

It's not easy – and it doesn't all happen in one go. Zen has the image of falling down seven times and getting up eight times. This is the kind of resilience we need to discover who we truly are.

For one thing, it's very easy to get distracted. Bowie committed to beginning the process in 1976 and continued with the program for the next half-dozen years. However, he then became extremely distracted from his process of self-discovery due to the most unfortunate circumstances: he became a global superstar.

Although during the 1970s Bowie was arguably the most important and influential figure in popular culture, he was never in commercial terms a true superstar. But in 1983 his *Let's Dance* album became a huge global seller. The album went to number one in many countries around the world and sold 10 million copies; the Serious Moonlight tour to promote the album – originally scheduled to play in 5000- to 10,000-seater venues – ended up touring stadiums of up to 80,000, with demand for tickets sometimes exceeding venue capacity by up to four times. By the middle of 1984 Bowie was quantifiably a ten times bigger star than he had been eighteen months earlier.

We know from his 1975 song 'Fame' that he didn't much like celebrity when he was only a cult success. This time round he was a global superstar – and the experience completely derailed him.

It wasn't that Bowie didn't want to be famous *at all*. A part of him was clearly attracted by the idea. Having found a big global audience, and specifically a major audience in the US, Bowie made compromises to hold on to them. He later described his behaviour during this period as 'pandering' to an audience whom he didn't recognize or understand, saying he would look out across the stadium audiences and wonder how many Velvet Underground albums 'these people' owned.

To hold onto this level of success he had to stop behaving like an outsider artist and instead behave like a celebrity. As he put it, 'there's a line the Americans won't cross. There has to be a certain conformity to things… whereas the English will embrace eccentrics.' All the eccentricity – as well as any hint of bisexuality – was furiously ironed out of Bowie's image throughout the mid-1980s as he created a new, squeaky-clean persona for the global and American audience.

His next two albums – *Tonight* and *Never Let Me Down* – sold well and led to another global stadium tour, but they were dull, uninspired and left Bowie (who described them as 'disastrous') feeling disappointed in himself, uncomfortable and unhappy with his life. Looking back on the period later, he was appalled at the lack of integrity in his actions and saw with clarity how fame had become a hindrance and an obstacle to pursuing his true purpose.

He was selling albums, he was making money but the price of this career and financial success was that he had put his spiritual quest on hold. His journey to discover himself was sabotaged by this new mainstream-friendly persona. He reached the stage where he began to think of simply making as much money as he could quickly from this sudden success and then retiring: 'I thought I was obviously just an empty vessel and would end up like everyone else doing these stupid fucking shows singing "Rebel Rebel" until I fall over and bleed.'

It's perhaps characteristic of Bowie's life that the period many people see as his greatest triumph was a period of deep unhappiness. Equally, the period in his career that most people consider the biggest disaster was for him a joy and a blessing.

EVERYTHING YOU KNOW IS WRONG

Neither the critics nor Bowie's fans – nor anyone else for that matter – really liked Tin Machine, the band Bowie put together as an escape route from his period of mega-fame, but Bowie considered it the best thing that could possibly have happened to him.

The idea of Tin Machine was that Bowie wasn't a solo artist any more; instead, he was just 'one of the band'. Inevitably, this bid for anonymity failed and all the attention remained on Bowie. But this (admittedly slightly artificial) abandonment of his expected career path meant Bowie relearned what it meant to simply write what he wanted, rather than to meet an audience's expectations, and this reminded him of what he really wanted to do: to be an experimental artist committed to constantly exploring new areas, not just a pop star desperately looking for a sound that the public liked:

> Tin Machine was very important because it decontextualized me. After that nobody had any idea what I was supposed to be.

And he kept people guessing throughout the 1990s with a string of albums that wilfully changed style and direction. If you liked one Bowie album in the 1990s, there was no guarantee that you would like the next one. It became increasingly hard to work out who 'Bowie's audience' was, but Bowie was becoming increasingly clear about who *he* was. It was during this period that he took further steps to tackle his addictive behaviour by joining Alcoholics Anonymous. Crucially, it was also during this period that he met and married Iman (more of this in Chapter 9).

In 2002 Bowie released the album *Heathen*. If we might argue that in 1977 on *Low* and *Heroes* Bowie finally began to discover who David Bowie was, we might also argue that on *Heathen* Bowie made a major step forward in the process of discovering who David Jones was.

On an American talk show, promoting the album, Bowie said: 'I think this may be the most intimate album I've ever made. This one is not about anybody else other than myself and how I feel about things.' It's a quote that many singer-songwriters could apply to every album they make. But for Bowie, who had spent years hiding away from how he felt about things, it's an extraordinary pronouncement reflecting a genuine change. Bowie was finally happy in his own skin.

So what lies behind this shift in perspective on *Heathen*? What had Bowie been thinking about? What ideas had he been exploring? Bowie gave us some clues on the album artwork, which includes pictures of three books: Freud's *Interpretation of Dreams*, Einstein's *The General Theory of Relativity*, and Nietzsche's *The Gay Science*. These are three extraordinary works (there is not an actual book by Einstein titled *The General Theory of Relativity*, but he did publish *Foundations of the General Theory of Relativity* in 1916, a year after his initial papers on the theory were published in academic journals). They tell us that our world is not as we think it is (Einstein) and that we are not as we think we are (Freud and Nietzsche). Bowie's summation of the cumulative message of these three works was that: 'Everything we'd known before was wrong. Everything.'

THE LIFE LESSON: KEEP SEARCHING TILL YOU FIND YOUR TRUE SELF

At this stage in our search for our self we need to contemplate the idea that perhaps we don't have a self at all. It's time to explore (and perhaps embrace) the Buddhist concept of 'no self' – not simply to be contrary, but because exploring the concept of no self may prove central to finding more happiness in your life.

Among the iconoclastic ideas in *The Gay Science* is Nietzsche's famous proclamation that 'God is dead'. Although it is rarely easy to be 100 per cent clear exactly what Nietzsche is saying (this quotation is actually spoken, Nietzsche tells us, by 'a madman'), this statement and his subsequent discussion of morality are often interpreted to mean that we can no longer depend on a list of 'thou shalts' and 'thou shalt nots' – an objective, shared moral code – to guide us through life, and must instead look inside ourselves to establish our own set of values. We will go through this process in the *Your Path* section of this chapter.

Arguably, however, 'God is dead' is not the most iconoclastic statement in Nietzsche's philosophy; that may be his belief that our sense of self is an illusion.

When Bowie was striving to be himself – and the song 'Heroes' is as much about Bowie's own psychological struggle as it is anything else – three distinct ideas that he had long since absorbed and referenced in his work (Western psychology, Buddhism and the philosophy of Nietzsche) would all have been urging him to question the very idea of self. Each of these traditions states that our self is not what we commonly think it is, and each comes up with a slightly different view of what it actually is.

As we saw in the previous chapter, Western psychology suggests our regular concept of our self is incomplete: there is more hidden beneath the surface. It emphasizes the need to integrate previously rejected aspects of the unconscious in order to fully realize the self.

Of the three works pictured on *Heathen*'s artwork, it is Nietzsche's book that was the most potent for Bowie. By this time, Bowie had been fascinated by Nietzsche's work for more than thirty years. Nietzsche claimed in *The Gay Science* that 'everyone is furthest from himself', emphasizing the difficulty of self-discovery. His equivalent of the journey of self-realization is the quest to become the Übermensch – the Overman. Human beings reach the desired state of Overman, Nietzsche tells us, by 'seeing through the illusion of the self'.

Buddhism goes one step further, declaring simply that there is no such thing as self at all.

At which point, you are entitled to wonder if any of this matters. Couldn't we just leave the philosophers to their abstract concepts and get on with our lives?

Well, we could. But the danger is that – if they're right – the lives we get on with won't be our real lives. We'll be missing out on the true experience of living. Alan Watts, the author of *The Way of Zen*, a book Bowie devoured as a teenager, was a brilliant explainer of complex Eastern philosophies. He has a typically elegant metaphor to explain why we should try to understand tricky concepts like no self: because if we don't, we will go through our lives 'eating the menu' instead of the food. We will experience not the vivid, wonderful reality of life itself but a diluted version of reality filtered through our conceptual thought. We will live in the map not in the territory.

So what am I asking you to do? To strengthen your sense of your self – as Western psychology would advise? Or to let it go completely – as Buddhism would urge you to do?

Unless… there couldn't possibly be any way that we could do both, could there? I think there might be. But before we can find out, we'll need to get our heads around one more intriguing aspect of Buddhist philosophy: the idea that there are two realities.

And oddly, when we look at this 2500-year-old philosophical idea, we will find we are also staring straight at the world of quantum mechanics in which Einstein's theories play a vital role.

MOUNTAINS ARE NO LONGER MOUNTAINS, TREES ARE NO LONGER TREES

Both Buddhism and Nietzsche agree that the reality we live in isn't half as real as we think it is. In fact, Nietzsche makes the typically grand claim that *all* philosophies must conclude that this is so. In *Beyond Good and Evil* he writes, 'whatever standpoint of philosophy we may adopt today; from every point of view the erroneousness of the world in which we believe we live is the surest and firmest thing we can get our eyes on'.

Buddhism states that the world we usually think we live in is *relative* reality; beyond this, as you attain deeper understanding, you will be able to see *absolute* reality (the 'real' reality, if you will).

To explain this, Bowie's teacher Chime Rinpoche sometimes used the Zen saying that before you begin meditating, 'mountains are mountains and trees are trees': that is, you see the world in the usual way. After you have meditated for a while, you realize that 'mountains are no longer mountains and trees are no longer trees': that is, you see the absolute reality in which all things are interconnected rather than separate. If you continue to practise meditation, the Zen saying maintains, you reach a point when 'mountains are again mountains, and trees are again trees': that is, you retain your deeper understanding of absolute reality, and this deeper awareness of the interconnectedness of all things allows you to function more skilfully in the relative reality of your everyday life. You live in the same relative reality as the rest of us, but all your actions are informed by your knowledge of absolute reality.

It's not easy to get our heads around the idea that the reality we can observe through our senses isn't true and that there is another more accurate reality out there. However, it's easier to get our heads around it now than it used to be because science has already explained to us something equally at odds with the way we perceive reality: that the solid objects all around us aren't solid at all, but are in fact collections of very many incredibly small, incredibly fast-moving things zooming around in space; and that, in each of the apparently solid objects we can perceive, there is far more space than there is object. And yet, I'm still tapping away at solid keys on a solid keyboard resting securely on a solid desk, sitting on a solid chair on a solid floor.

When we discover this is what modern physics tells us, we think something like, 'Well, it doesn't look that way and it certainly doesn't feel that way, but... OK, I guess it could be true.' And we accept it – even if we're not sure we truly understand it.

In a very similar way, we can take this idea of absolute reality – the idea that we are all connected, not separate – and say, 'Well, it doesn't look that way and it certainly doesn't feel that way, but... OK, I guess it could be true.' And we can accept it – even if we're not sure we truly understand it.

In fact, isn't Buddhism simply saying the same thing as physics? Or, to put the right chronology on that, isn't physics just saying the same thing as Buddhism? Surely the message of modern physics is essentially: first chairs are chairs and desks are desks, but if you carry out our experiments, you will see that chairs are not chairs and desks are not desks. But once you know this, of course, the best way to navigate your day is to work on the basis that the chair is a chair and the desk is a desk. That way, you know where to sit and what to put your mug of tea on.

If any physicists are reading this, yes, I'm aware that my description of an atom as a 'small thing' is far from accurate. Atoms might be small but as no less an authority than Werner Heisenberg, the German theoretical physicist and winner of the

Nobel prize, has pointed out, 'atoms are not things'. Heisenberg tells us: 'the atoms or the elementary particles... form a world of potentialities or possibilities rather than one of things or facts'. Indeed, the pioneers of quantum modern physics tell us exactly the same message as the Buddhists: stop thinking about the world as a collection of things, stop seeing the world as a lot of separate bits.

> What is needed is for man to give attention to his habit of fragmentary thought, to be aware of it, and thus bring it to an end. Man's approach to reality may then be whole.

This is a comment from the theoretical physicist, David Bohm. However, it could easily be a quote from the Buddha or one of the Zen masters who issue koans to help their students understand that the way they think doesn't correspond to reality. Bohm, by the way, is best known for his theory of implicate and explicate order, which states (wait for it...) that there are two realities: the observable reality that we are aware of and a deeper reality that lies beyond. His theory was developed to explain the behaviour of subatomic particles – but it resonates strongly with the 2500-year-old Eastern philosophy of two realities.

We will now explore the concept of no self, not just because it sounds intriguing but because there will be a benefit to us at the end of our exploration. And now that we understand the Zen saying about mountains and trees, we know that it is safe to explore the concept of no self because we will not lose our hard-earned sense of self. We understand that, even if at some point we decide there is no self, we will be able to move on to a further position where once again there is a self. We will just have a slightly – but crucially – different perspective on it.

NO SELF, NO PROBLEM

The first sense in which Buddhists talk about there being no self is probably the easiest to understand: the idea that there is no *fixed* self.

We all change constantly. We can see that we physically change, and we know – if we've done any science at school – that our body will end up being made of very different atoms than the ones that made us when we were born. We are in constant flux.

We know that our beliefs and opinions change too. On this point Nietzsche concurs with Buddhist thought: 'At any given moment, you are a different person,' he wrote in *The Gay Science*. So how can we 'become who we are'? Nietzsche might suggest that becoming is a never-ending process. His Overman, like the enlightened Buddhist, is totally at home with uncertainty and continuing change.

A second sense in which Buddhists say there is no self is that there is *no one in charge*. There is not a single boss inside your head.

We first mentioned this in Chapter 1. Having now been through the work in Chapter 5 (where we came to understand that we do not actively generate our thoughts, but instead most of our thoughts just happen to us), it should now be easier to understand what this means. There is not one central, controlling chief executive in charge of everything you do.

When you sit in meditation and try to focus on your breath but instead are assailed by a never-ending stream of thoughts, feelings and other distractions, it seems as if there are dozens of competing bits of software running inside you, all with their own needs, wants and priorities, all throwing up thoughts and feelings.

A third sense in which the Buddhists say there is no self is that there is no *separate* self, that we are intrinsically linked to everybody else and everything else in the world. This is probably the hardest aspect of no self for us to comprehend – because again it seems so different from the world as we perceive it. But having opened up to the fact that the world of subatomic particles is completely different than the way we perceive the world of desks and chairs and yet is real, for now let's hold on to the possibility that this might be true as well.

I want you to do this because it matters, because our sense of being separate is the root of so much of our suffering, our anxiety, our alienation, our angst and indeed our anger. Grasp this aspect of no self, and so much misery – our feeling that we don't belong, our feeling that there is something missing in our lives – starts to dissipate.

Let's go back to Alan Watts – favourite author of the teenage David Bowie. There is no clearer explanation of no self than his book *The Book on the Taboo Against Knowing Who You Are* in which he says that 'the prevalent sensation of oneself as a separate ego enclosed in a bag of skin is a hallucination which accords neither with Western science nor with the experimental philosophy-religions of the East'. He writes:

> We suffer from an hallucination, from a false and distorted sensation of our own existence... Most of us have the sensation that 'I myself' is a separate center of feeling and action, living inside and bounded by the physical body – a center which 'confronts' an 'external' world of people and things, making contact through the senses with a universe both alien and strange. Everyday figures of speech reflect this illusion. 'I came into this world.' 'You must face reality.' 'The conquest of nature.' This feeling of being lonely and very temporary visitors in the universe is in flat contradiction to everything known about man (and all other living organisms) in the sciences. We do not 'come into' this world; we come out of it, as leaves from a tree. As the ocean 'waves', the universe 'peoples'. Every individual is an expression of the whole realm of nature, a unique action of the total universe.

This shift in perception – to see yourself as intrinsically *part* of the universe, an action of the universe, rather than some strange separate thing dumped *into* the universe – is potentially transformative. If you can truly grasp this, you have the option of treating life as a 'fabulous game', says Watts, rather than as a separate thing that you are supposed to get something out of 'as if life were a bank to be robbed'.

We noted earlier that Buddhism claims attachment as the root cause of suffering but, without a self, there can be no attachment. The more strongly we hold on to our sense of ourselves as *separate* selves – in opposition to the universe around us – the more solid our problems become. The more we can inch our way towards the idea of no self – towards an understanding of ourselves as interconnected aspects of the universe – the more we can begin to shed the unnecessary layers of mental suffering that humans seem to be plagued with.

The mindfulness teacher Jack Kornfield tells of a time when he asked a Sri Lankan meditation master to tell him the essence of Buddhism. The master laughed and said three times.

> No self, no problem.
>
> No self, no problem.
>
> No self, no problem.

Can we somehow have the strong sense of self that Western psychology advises, while at the same time holding that sense of self very lightly indeed, as Eastern philosophy urges us to do? Is that even remotely possible? I believe it is. I believe that if we can get to a point where we see that mountains are not mountains and trees are not trees, and then come back to a place where mountains are mountains and trees are trees, then equally we can reach an understanding of no self but come back to a place where on a day-to-day basis our self exists.

There are stories of the Buddha being challenged on the idea of 'no self' – being asked, essentially, 'So is it true that we don't have a self?' Typically, Buddha's response was along the lines of: 'Don't even ask. Don't get caught up in such theorizing. It doesn't help.' What is clear is that – as with so many Buddhist teachings – the idea of no self is not a 'truth'. Debating the veracity of the concept is irrelevant.

No self is not a doctrine. It is a *strategy for living.*

So let's choose to see it like that. Rather than think there are perhaps just a very special few who somehow achieve the rare enlightened state of living permanently as no self, let's consider instead that perhaps we can all gradually move slowly towards it, that it can be a gradual shift of perspective that we undertake as a strategy for letting go of suffering, letting go of the causes of suffering and embracing life in a new fuller way that opens up the possibility of more happiness.

Buddha was not interested in 'the serpentine dance of dragons' – whether something was true or false, right or wrong, verifiable or not; as ever, his primary concern was 'does it work?' and 'will it help?' It can do. It might help you. Let's find out how to get at least a glimpse of what no self might feel like.

YOUR PATH

In this section you will both strengthen your sense of self through some thorough work on your values, and also prepare to let go of your sense of self altogether with some deeper meditative work. Does that sound odd? Perhaps it is. But here we go anyway…

Meditation has been important throughout this book. At this point it becomes absolutely vital. It's hard to fully grasp ideas like Chapter 5's 'you are not your thoughts' without meditating. It is even harder to fully grasp this chapter's idea of no self without a regular meditation practice.

Even with regular meditation, you cannot reach a sense of no self at will. It is not something you can attain. It is something that happens to you. You can, however, get yourself into a state of preparedness in which it is more likely to happen.

As with all meditation, intention is key. Or, perhaps more accurately, lack of intention is key. Actively trying to make anything happen will not help your meditation; the less you try – or hope – to reach a sense of no self, the more likely it is to happen.

Although this seems infuriatingly perverse, it is the truth. At the heart of meditation – and it is one of the most important benefits of meditation – is the fact that this is perhaps the one single activity in your life when you are not trying to achieve anything.

The attributes we are encouraged to bring to meditation include non-striving or non-doing. In a sense, at the very moment when we remove the idea of any desired outcome, we have begun the process of uncovering no self. Our conventional self has very strong opinions about what it wants, and for the most part it wants something other than what it has. Our conventional self wants something to happen, wants to do something, wants to get somewhere, wants to tick an item off the to-do list. When we sit in a state that involves none of these desires, we are removing many of the ways in which our self makes itself known.

If you don't want anything, don't want to do anything, don't want anything in particular to happen, the sense of a 'you' is very unimportant. What would it be needed for? While you are meditating, your sense of self is hardly needed at all.

Having said all this, how does a sense of no self happen?

In the meditations in this book, I have instructed you to focus on the breath. This is the start point. If you meditate for a reasonable period of time, and if you can successfully stay focused on the breath, you will become increasingly tuned in to the rhythm of the breath. As more time elapses, a change in perception can sometimes occur: you become *one* with the breath. What does that mean? It means that you are still aware that breathing is happening, but there is no longer any sense that there is a 'you' who is doing the breathing.

It doesn't have to be the breath that leads you to no self. It could be simple awareness. You can sit in simple awareness of whatever is happening – sounds, physical sensations, thoughts – and over time, again, you may experience a similar shift in perspective: awareness is still continuing but there is no sense any more that there is a 'you' who is aware. But I would suggest that using the breath as a specific focus is probably the easiest route to no self. There is something about the regular rhythm of the breath that encourages a letting-go.

Your task is to get rid of the meditator and simply allow there to be meditation happening. Except it isn't a task because it's not something you could aim for. You simply leave yourself open to the possibility.

Let's meditate again now – not, given everything we've just said, with the specific intention of attaining no self but simply to explore the idea of going further into the breath.

Exercise: Definitely not a no self meditation

As with previous meditations, sit in a state of relaxed alertness, keeping the spine straight, but allowing the shoulders to let go.

Close your eyes.

Take a few moments to acknowledge that you have slowed down and actively chosen to take a pause in your day. And then become aware of any sounds that you can hear. After a few moments, switch your focus away from the sounds to your breath.

Notice your breath at any place in your body – at any point in the breathing process – that makes the most sense to you. It may be at the nostrils as the air enters the nose. It may be at the back of the throat. It may be in the chest as it rises and falls or in the belly as that rises and falls. For a while, simply stay with this specific focus on one area of the breath, noting the in breath and the out breath.

As thoughts arise, which they inevitably will, notice them, label them as thinking and let them go. Then gently, without any judgement over the fact that you have been distracted, return your attention to the breath.

Over time, broaden your focus away from one specific area to instead follow the whole process of the breath.

Follow the journey of the air entering your nose, travelling down the back of your throat and filling the lungs.

Become aware of every cubic centimetre of expansion in your body as it happens.

Notice the end of the in breath. Allow, and be aware of, a brief pause. Then notice the very beginning of contraction as the out breath begins. Follow the journey of the whole out breath.

As thoughts arise again, which they will, notice them, label them and let them go. If you start to become bored, notice this as just another thought. Label it 'thinking that I'm bored', and let it go. Continue with the meditation.

Simply follow the whole journey of the in breath and the out breath. Do this for as long as you can.

Repeat this meditation as often as you can. The longer you meditate and the more regularly you meditate, the deeper the meditation will become. At some point there may be a shift in perception. It's hard to put into words. But there will simply be breathing and meditation, there will not be somebody breathing or somebody meditating. Don't try to *make* this happen – that would pretty much guarantee that it won't.

It's an elusive state, and if it happens, it may not last long. But even a brief, occasional glimpse of this other state may be enough to help you approach life differently: as a fabulous game, not as a bank to be robbed. So it may well be worth the fairly lengthy time commitment.

Remember: 'No self, no problem. No self, no problem. No self, no problem.'

Exercise: Identifying and checking your values

Look at the list of values printed opposite, and choose those you believe are most important to you in your life and that help guide the way you live. I would suggest you choose between three and five, but feel free to choose more if you think they are relevant.

Once you have selected your values, do the following four things for each one.

1. Think of an example from your own life when you truly lived up to this value – a moment when your actions or words brought this value to life.

Acceptance
Accountability
Achievement
Adventurous
Appreciation
Authenticity
Autonomy

Balance
Belonging
Benevolence
Boldness

Calmness
Caring
Charity
Cheerfulness
Cleverness
Collaboration
Community
Commitment
Compassion
Consistency
Contribution
Cooperation
Courtesy
Creativity
Credibility
Curiosity

Decisiveness
Dedication
Dependability
Discipline
Diversity

Efficient
Empathy
Encouragement
Enthusiasm
Ethics
Excellence

Fairness
Family
Flexibility
Friendships
Freedom
Fun

Generosity
Grace
Gratitude
Growth

Happiness
Hard-working
Health
Honesty
Humility
Humour

Inclusiveness
Independence
Individuality
Innovation
Inspiration

Joy
Justice

Kindness
Knowledge

Leadership
Learning
Love
Loyalty

Making a difference
Mindfulness

Optimism
Open-mindedness
Originality

Passion
Personal development
Peace
Playfulness
Preparedness
Positivity
Proactivity
Professionalism
Punctuality

Quality

Recognition
Relationships
Reliability
Resilience
Resourcefulness
Respect
Responsibility
Results-oriented

Security
Self-control
Selflessness
Service
Simplicity
Spirituality
Stability
Success

Thoughtfulness
Tolerance
Traditionalism
Trustworthiness
Truth

Understanding
Usefulness
Versatility
Vision
Warmth
Wealth
Well-being
Wisdom

2. Think of an example from your life when you failed to live up to this value – when what you did or what you said were inconsistent with this value.
3. Think of a moment when you have seen somebody else live up to this value (or a value very like it). If you cannot think of any examples from real life, examples from fiction – books, films, plays – can be used.
4. Think of an example when you have seen somebody else behave in a way that is opposite to this value or in a way that would offend or upset somebody who holds this value.

Having thought about these four examples, now review your list. Do you still believe they are the right values for you? Do you want to remove any from the list or add any new ones?

Exercise: Understanding your values

Having confirmed that these are your values, answer the following questions for each one.

> *Why is this value important to you?* For example, if your value is self-discipline, your answer might be: 'Because I want to be the best person I can be, and without self-discipline I know that I lapse into behaviours that do not reflect this.'
>
> *What are the beliefs you hold that support this value or lead you to having this value?* For example, if your value is

respect, your beliefs might include: 'I believe everyone is entitled to be treated with respect.'

What do you do in your daily life that shows that this is one of your values? For example, if your value is collaboration, your answer might include: 'When I run a meeting at work I always make sure to ask everyone individually for their input.'

For each value, write a sentence that begins 'I want to…' and brings the value to life or explains how the value fits into your life. For example, if your value is fairness, your sentence might be: 'I want to promote fairness and equality in every community I am involved in.'

Having gone through all these exercises, take another moment to review your list of values and again confirm that you believe they are the right list. Feel free at this point to remove one or more, or to add one or more new ones. This is work in progress.

Exercise: Tiny tweaks

Having confirmed your values, now set these aside for a week. At the end of each day during that week, monitor what happened:

Were there any occasions where you lived up to any of your values?

Were there any occasions where you could have lived up to one of your values but failed to do so?

Allow yourself to be honest in the second category. There is no shame in failing to live up to your values occasionally. We all do it.

At the end of the week, having reviewed the times when you aligned with your values and when you failed to do so, set yourself the task of coming up with one tiny tweak that you could make to your life that would make you better able to align with each value.

These are not huge behavioural changes. These are very simple things you can do that would make it easier to live up to your values. For example, if your value is gratitude your tiny tweak could be: 'I will buy some thank-you cards and keep them on my desk where I can see them with a supply of envelopes and stamps. A thank-you email is nice but a handwritten note is rare these days and even more special.'

Exercise: Write about your values

Writing about your values on an ongoing basis will help you to live aligned to your values and will also have greater benefits. In her book *The Upside of Stress*, psychologist Kelly McGonigal states that, 'writing about your values is one of the most effective psychological interventions ever studied', noting that journaling about personal values, 'makes people feel more powerful, in control, proud and strong. It also makes them feel more loving, connected and empathetic towards others. It increases pain tolerance, enhances self-control and reduces unhelpful rumination after a stressful experience.'

It's an impressive list of benefits. How exactly does writing about values do all that? The theory is that, in writing about your personal values and how they have connected to the events in your life, you are able to unpack and clarify the meaning behind what happens to you – especially life's more stressful events. It's one thing to be exhausted after a long day. It's another thing to take a moment to understand that the reason you're exhausted is because you went out of your way to help a friend in line with your value of friendship. A day that you might have dismissed as simply tiring or a day when 'things were too much for me' has instead become a day that has real meaning for you as a day when you dug deep and rose to the challenge to help a friend in line with your values.

Your path: Going forward

1. Continue to meditate. Incorporate the deeper focus on the breath featured in the *Definitely not a no self meditation* featured earlier in this section.

2. Do you think that self/no self is like an on/off switch? Or is it more of a spectrum? Do you think that during your meditation you have noticed a gradual lessening of the sense of self? Has the sense of 'you' that you carry with you through the rest of the day become slightly less important during meditation?

3. Try committing to spend a certain part of each day with no personal agenda. During this period allow others to dictate your schedule, do what everyone else wants to do, listen to what others have to say without

contradicting, correcting or one-upping them. Do not try to achieve anything for your own benefit. Do this for as long as you can manage. The longer the better.

4. Spend the next week pondering the question: 'Who am I if I have no self?' If that is too abstract for you, bring it down a notch and live with one of these questions instead: 'Who am I if I have no fixed self?' 'Who am I if I am not separate from the rest of the universe?' If that is still a little too out there, try spending the next week regularly asking yourself: 'How would I experience this situation differently if I held my sense of self much more lightly?'

CHAPTER 9: LOVE

The life lesson: Always stay open to love

There have been periods in my life when I have been so closeted in my own world that I would no longer relate to anybody… These days, more than ever, I feel like a very social animal, which I wasn't at one time. And I love the freedom of it. I love the joy it brings.

(David Bowie)

To live is to love. To love nothing is to be dead. To be happy is to devote oneself. To exist only for oneself is to cast oneself away, and to exile oneself in hell.

(Eliphas Levi, The Keys of the Mysteries*)*

Love, too, has to be learned.

(Frederick Nietzsche, The Gay Science*)*

BOWIE'S PATH

In the late 1980s Bowie finally looked beneath the 'David Bowie' mask to find the real David Jones. The catalyst for this deeper self-examination and greater personal honesty was falling in love with Iman. Before this, Bowie could not love. Finally letting go of his need for control and opening himself up to love led to the happiness of his later years.

In Chapter 2, we examined Bowie's interview with Mavis Nicholson on the daytime TV show *Afternoon Plus* in 1979. We learned that, as a child, he didn't have a teddy bear or any such soft toy and that he never liked children's things very much. Pressed to think of a childhood influence, he landed on Donald Duck. Did he *like* Donald Duck? No, he couldn't stand him. Donald Duck was important, Bowie said, because he 'made me learn how to hate'.

The interview, then, offers a revealing glimpse into Bowie's cold childhood. It also tells us much more. Let's now examine another part of their conversation as they talk about love and also reference one of the most important moments in Bowie's teenage years – a traumatic incident that is often downplayed in accounts of his life.

Many people know the story behind David Bowie's mismatched eyes: the fact that he was punched in the face by a school friend,

George Underwood, in a row over a girl and that, as a result, his pupil became paralyzed open. Bowie and Underwood remained friends. Indeed, Bowie later hired Underwood to provide artwork for the covers of *Hunky Dory* and *Ziggy Stardust*. And, of course, Bowie's distinctive eyes came to be seen as a cool part of his alien/outsider image. This has led many to underestimate the traumatic effect of an injury that led to two eye surgeries, several weeks in hospital and a permanent loss of visual perspective for the rest of his life. (Things, Bowie later explained, don't move towards him; they just get bigger.)

In the *Afternoon Plus* interview, Nicholson questions Bowie about love. Initially, Bowie breezily claims that he falls in love quite easily and quickly. Until, that is, Nicholson challenges him over what love truly means. At this point, Bowie's body language immediately becomes more defensive and closed, as if he is pushing the subject away from himself.

> Mavis: Once you love somebody it means you've got to share your life with them.
>
> David: No, I don't think so. I think you can love somebody from afar.
>
> Mavis: But if you then decided not to love them from afar, you – as an artist – would have to give up quite a lot of your time for them.
>
> David: Yes, and I can't do that. No, love can't get quite in my way… *[He holds both hands out in front of him – in a gesture to defend himself and to ward love off.]* because I feel… um… I shelter myself from it incredibly. *[He runs*

both hands up and down his body to suggest a layer of protection or armour.]

Mavis: What are you sheltering yourself against?

David: From losing that other eye.

At this point Bowie laughs, but it is a very nervous laugh. It's a joke but it's also very clearly *not* a joke.

In one of Bowie's favourite novels, Saul Bellow's *Herzog*, the eponymous hero writes a note saying, 'Not able to stand kindness at this time. Feelings, heart, everything in strange condition.' It could be a note written by Bowie at any point in the first half of his life, when love was not allowed to 'get in my way'.

Emotions, his family had told him, were 'only fit for the servants' quarters'. It would be reasonable to conclude that both his parents were, as a psychologist would say, poor resonators – unable to convey their own emotions clearly to the child or to reflect back accurately any emotions the child felt. As such, it is unsurprising that Bowie as a young man preferred not to express emotions at all.

In his book *Rebel Rebel*, the writer Chris O'Leary analyzes Bowie's song 'Station to Station', noting that when Bowie sings the word love he 'croaks' it out 'as if he's so unaware of [love] that he can't conceive of how to properly say the word'. Indeed, the year in which Bowie recorded 'Station to Station', he told *Playboy*:

> Never have been in love, to speak of. I was in love once maybe and it was an awful experience. It rotted me, drained me, and it was a disease. Hateful thing it was. Being in love is something that breeds brute anger and jealousy, everything but love, it seems.

It's easy then to believe accounts of Bowie's cold, emotionless, robot-like character during the early 1970s – such as the opinion of Ian Hunter, the lead singer of Mott the Hoople. It's worth remembering that Bowie was a fan of Mott the Hoople and an admirer of Hunter, and that he wrote a song for them – 'All the Young Dudes', which gave them their biggest hit, leading to a run of successful singles that finally garnered Hunter the respect his own talent deserved. And yet, despite all that Bowie had done for his band, Hunter described him like this: 'He never had humanity. He sucks. Like Dracula. He sucks what he can get. And then he moves on to another victim.'

Wow. If this is the impression that Bowie left on people he admired and helped, it is perhaps not surprising that during an interview in the *NME*, journalist Angus MacKinnon noted, 'Bowie positively leaks loneliness. It wraps itself around him like a clammy shroud.'

REJOINING THE HUMAN RACE

In 1996, when Bowie uttered the words about finally becoming a social animal that open this chapter, the journalist he was talking to – Mick Brown of the *Telegraph* – noted, 'It's almost as if you were hearing someone talking about rejoining the human race.'

This is exactly what Bowie was doing. The process of rejoining the human race began when Bowie discarded his final persona – the mainstream entertainer of the *Let's Dance/Tonight/Never Let Me Down* era – and formed the band Tin Machine. By any conventional measure the band was not a success, but it gave Bowie back to himself; and this meant he was ready for the meeting that was going to change his life.

In September 1990, knowing that Bowie was fascinated by the model Iman, his hairstylist Teddy Antolin invited her to his birthday party and then begged the still largely reclusive Bowie to attend too. We can't avoid the cliché: it was love at first sight.

Iman Mohamed Abdulmajid was not your average model. She was born in 1955, in Mogadishu, Somalia, and raised there until her father became ambassador to Saudi Arabia. Iman was sent to boarding school in more liberal Egypt, where she learned four languages (Arabic, Italian, French and English), but her education was interrupted in 1969 when she was fourteen, when her father was ordered to return to Somalia following a military coup. The family fled to Kenya, where Iman went on to study political science at the University of Nairobi. When a photographer stopped her in the street and asked if she'd ever considered modelling, Iman showed both her quick thinking and a strong sense of her own self-worth when she told him he could take pictures of her for $8000 – the cost of her tuition.

The photographer, Peter Beard, agreed and sent the photographs to the US. Iman's modelling career was launched. From 1975 to 1989 she was one of the world's top supermodels, but then she took the decision to retire. Knowing there was a new generation coming up behind her, she said she opted to 'leave with grace'. She also had a plan in place: to launch a line of cosmetics designed to reflect a more diverse range of skin colours than were catered for at that time.

So when they met, both Bowie and Iman were at transitional points in their lives – both, in a sense, stepping back from global fame to get a new perspective on their lives. As a result, both had the time and space to allow a new relationship into their lives. Crucially, Bowie – the man who fifteen years before had complained that love 'rotted' him – was finally ready to tear down the protective layers of armour he had constructed around his emotions.

Together Bowie and Iman achieved that rarity in the entertainment business: a long, stable, loving marriage.

ARE WE HAPPY NOW?

With Iman, Bowie was finally able to open himself up to love – a significant shift in his life. This was reflected both in his work and in the fact that he became much more comfortable talking about his emotions.

In 1992, a year after their marriage, Bowie released *Black Tie White Noise*. He told *Rolling Stone* that the new album came from a very different emotional place, which reflected: 'a willingness to relinquish full control over my emotions, let them go a bit, start relating to other people, which is something that's been happening to me slowly – and, my God, it's been uphill – over the last ten or twelve years'.

My God, it *had* been uphill, but he was now on course. He continued: 'I feel a lot freer these days to be able to talk about myself and about what's happened to me, because I've been able to face it. For many years, everything was always blocked out. The day before was always blocked out. I never wanted to return to examine anything that I did particularly. But the stakes have changed. I feel alive, in a real sense.'

By the time of his 1999 album *Hours*, Bowie was able to say simply that the album was about love. That's all. No aliens, no concepts, no characters. Just love. The thing that he had had to defend himself against, the thing he used to consider 'a disease', the word that he could previously hardly pronounce – now he could write a whole album about it.

As part of the PR launch of *Hours*, Bowie wrote an intriguing interview with his younger self that appeared in various publications around the world. One section went like this:

> David Bowie Jr: Are we happy now?
>
> David Bowie Sr: We're happier than we've ever been. More than we deserve really.
>
> David Bowie Jr: What do you mean by that?
>
> David Bowie Sr: It took you a long, long time to learn how to share your life with another person. We've just about got life in focus now.

Getting life in focus involved finally understanding not just the difference between David Bowie's personas and David Bowie, but also between David Bowie and David Jones. Achieving this meant that Iman was able to state with conviction: 'I fell in love with David Jones, I did not fall in love with David Bowie. David Bowie is just a persona... David Jones is a man I met.'

Cast your mind back to what we know of Bowie's childhood: no cuddly toys, and that strict 'don't make a mess' instruction when he got his paints out. Now compare this with Bowie's approach to parenting. When their daughter Lexi was a toddler, Iman revealed in a webchat with Bowie fans that Lexi most certainly did have toys to cuddle – her favourite was a doll called Puddles – and that proud father David allowed her to play happily and noisily on his musical instruments.

Having finally been able to open himself up to love, it is clear that Bowie, with Iman, was determined to give Lexi a very different childhood to the one he had: one in which a toddler could bash about on daddy's expensive guitars without being told off, and in which she had Puddles for cuddles.

THE LIFE LESSON: ALWAYS STAY OPEN TO LOVE

How can we let more love into our lives? First, we need to be sure that we know what love actually is. (Hint: it's not the 'I can't live without you' dependency depicted in so many love songs.) Then we need to know where to look for it.

Where did David Bowie go? He went into a wardrobe.

At the end of his last appearance, in the video for 'Lazarus', Bowie backed jerkily into a wardrobe and disappeared from our lives. He was dressed in an outfit identical to that in which he sketched the tree of life (in the photo session used on the cover of *Station to Station* reissues), so he clearly wanted to remind us how important the Jewish mysticism of the Kabbalah had been to him. But you can't really walk into a wardrobe (backwards or forwards) in our culture without implicitly referencing Narnia, the fantasy world explored in C. S. Lewis's children's books.

Bowie didn't throw his symbolism around lightly. Had he been rereading the Narnia books (all of which were originally published during Bowie's childhood) with their mix of Christian and pagan themes as his life drew to a close? Had he been reading C. S. Lewis more widely? Here's what C. S. Lewis had to say about love:

> There is no safe investment. To love at all is to be vulnerable. Love anything, and your heart will certainly be wrung and possibly be broken. If you want to make sure of keeping it intact, you must give your heart to no one, not even to an animal. Wrap it carefully round with hobbies and little luxuries; avoid all entanglements; lock it up safe in the casket or coffin of your selfishness.

In the first part of his life Bowie had tried this strategy and ended up – as Lewis predicted anyone who locked up their heart would – in hell. Realizing his fate, Bowie opted to open himself up again to love. How did he do that? How can any of us do that? How can we actively choose to cultivate love?

Some people use therapy to achieve this aim. You may think therapy is there to give insight into your problems. But as the writers of *A General Theory of Love* – Thomas Lewis, Fari Amini and Richard Lannon – put it, 'insight is the popcorn of therapy'. The journey of the patient and the therapist is the actual film. The authors say that people 'come to therapy unable to love and leave with that skill restored'.

So that is one option open to us if we want to reconnect with our ability to love. But, as far as we know, Bowie never went through therapy. He chose to make the journey back to love without such professional help. He did, of course, attend Alcoholics Anonymous meetings and we know that he heard there a message about relinquishing control and increasing acceptance, which resonated with him and will certainly have helped him reconnect with his emotions.

As we relinquish control, we open to connect with others. In *A General Theory of Love*, the patient–therapist relationship journey is described in this way: 'Those who succeed in revealing themselves to another find the dimness receding from their own visions of self. Like people awakening from a dream, they slough off the accumulated ill-fitting trappings of unsuitable lives.' This could potentially be *any* relationship. When we are truly seen by another, we can open.

We know remarkably little about the marriage of Bowie and Iman. In our celebrity obsessed world they managed somehow to keep the union of a rock god and a supermodel largely anonymous. We do not know what they gave each other or got from each other, but the fact that Bowie's journey to rejoin the human race coincided so closely with this relationship with Iman – well, it simply can't be just a coincidence. Instead we must assume that they had just such a mutually revealing relationship, learning about themselves as they learned about each other, each truly seeing and being seen by the other, and both growing emotionally within the marriage – and that, in this way, Bowie was able to 'slough off the accumulated ill-fitting trappings' of his previous way of life.

Am I going to suggest that every reader who wants to open up to love should marry a supermodel? It doesn't seem the most practical solution, does it? So what else was going on? What else might have helped Bowie open to love? And how can we learn to do the same?

LOVE STARTS WITH YOU

One of the key concepts taught by Chögyam Trungpa Rinpoche was *maitri*, so it's likely Bowie will have been introduced to the idea during his time at Samye Ling monastery. *Maitri* is the Sanskrit word meaning love, and the teachings centre around the idea that we must be kind, friendly and loving towards ourselves before we can love others. In the Pali language, the equivalent word is *metta*, and we meet the concept in modern mindfulness when we practise Metta Bhavana – otherwise known as a loving-kindness meditation.

If you have studied mindfulness and if you had a good teacher, you will have been introduced to a loving-kindness meditation as an extraordinarily powerful practice that will have helped you cultivate your capacity to love. If you had a less good teacher, you might have been introduced to the loving-kindness meditation as quite a fluffy New-Agey exercise in which smiling groups of people wish happiness to the whole world. In this form it's the kind of hippyish stuff that makes some people run a mile from mindfulness and meditation. This watered-down version of loving-kindness meditation (which focuses on the surface of the practice and doesn't explain what is supposed to be happening *beneath* the surface) leads to a significant misunderstanding of what the meditation is actually about.

Bhavana can be translated as meaning meditation, but here it means 'development' or 'cultivation'. In a loving-kindness meditation we are not, first and foremost, spreading love around the world; we are looking for it within ourselves. The real work of a loving-kindness meditation lies not in the nice act of wishing happiness to others but in the sometimes rather more difficult work of locating and cultivating the love within yourself first.

We'll go carefully through every stage of a loving-kindness meditation in the *Your Path* section, but before we can do that we need to understand exactly what cultivating love means – and before we can do that, we have to understand exactly what love means.

WHAT IS LOVE?

We all know what love is, don't we?

But *do* we? In Chapter 6 we clarified that, in the context of the work we are undertaking in this book, the word 'God' does not mean what many of us commonly assume it means. Within esoteric spiritual traditions 'God' means something different – and the distinction is vital. Similarly, we must be clear that the word 'love', when used in deep practices like a loving-kindness meditation, does not mean what many of us commonly assume it means. The love that we are discussing is crucially different from the way we may use the word in our day-to-day lives.

Our understanding of what love is tends to be shaped by two factors: the use of the word in popular culture (especially Hollywood films and pop songs), and the influence of capitalism on our behaviour. Thanks to capitalism, we have transformed ourselves and the other people in our lives into commodities. Not all of us, and not all the time, but to an alarming extent. When we look for a relationship, we do so in much the same way that we look for new clothes, a new phone or a new car. We are trying to secure the best product on the market that we can.

If, during his Berlin years, Bowie had left his apartment, hopped onto his Raleigh bike and – instead of heading north to the Hansa studios – cycled west for a few minutes, he would have come to Bayerischer Platz, once the haunt of Jewish artists and intellectuals. Einstein lived here, and later so did the psychoanalyst and social philosopher Erich Fromm. *The Art of Loving*, Fromm's enquiry into the nature of love, echoes Buddhist thought in talking of love as a 'skill' that can be learned and developed, and in placing emphasis on the need for the individual to first learn how to love themselves – not in a sense of conceit or arrogance or self-centredness, but as a prerequisite to being able to love the rest of the world. An individual can then form a genuinely loving relationship, in contrast to those who see supposedly loving relationships in capitalist terms:

> Modern man's happiness consists in the thrill of looking at the shop windows, and in buying all that he can afford to buy.... He (or she) looks at people in a similar way. For the man an attractive girl – and for the woman an attractive man – are the prizes they are after. 'Attractive' usually means a nice package of qualities which are popular and sought after on the personality market... The sense of falling in love develops usually only with regard to such human commodities as are within reach of one's own possibilities for exchange. I am out for a bargain; the object should be desirable from the standpoint of its social value, and at the same time should want me, considering my overt and hidden assets and potentialities. Two persons thus fall in love when they feel they have found the best

object available on the market, considering the limitations of their own exchange values.

That would have sounded cynical – even brutal – when Fromm wrote it in 1956 but, in the age of *Love Island* and Tinder, it seems to accurately describe the behaviour of a large proportion of the population.

The way we look at or evaluate a relationship is one factor that colours our understanding of the word 'love'; another is the assumption within our culture that love is something we have to go out and find in someone else, rather than something that we carry within us. We assume that if we want more love in our life, we have to find someone to love us. This is the version of love that we hear expressed most often in popular culture – typified by the 'I can't live without you' theme of so many love songs. Fromm would argue this is not love at all but rather 'symbiotic attachment' – a dysfunctional and damaging level of dependency.

Love in the sense that we use the word in a loving-kindness meditation is not primarily something that happens in a relationship with a specific person. It is a way of functioning in the world, which affects how we relate to everyone and everything.

Loving someone else is important, but in the context of the work we are doing here – the work of trying to open our heart to love – it is not our starting point. Finding someone to love and who will love us is an excellent idea, but if we want more love in our life, our first task is to find and develop the love within us. We have to learn how to love – or, perhaps more accurately, we have to learn how to become love. We have to open to the love that is already there.

Before we go looking for the object, we have to develop the ability.

CULTIVATING LOVE

Loving is a thing that we do naturally, but in many of us our ability to love has been blocked off or hampered. We have closed to love, but we can open again. This is the first task of the loving-kindness meditation: not to offer love to someone else, but to find it within ourselves and cultivate it.

The traditional Metta Bhavana consists of a series of aspirations. There are many variations of the wording, but they are all loosely based on a Buddhist chant called The Four Limitless Ones: 'May all sentient beings enjoy happiness and the root of happiness. May we be free from suffering and the root of suffering. May we not be separated from the great happiness devoid of suffering. May we dwell in the great equanimity free from passion, aggression, and prejudice.'

In a loving-kindness meditation, we say something like this: 'May X be happy and know the root of happiness. May X be free from suffering and the root of suffering. May X be safe and protected and free from harm. May X be healthy. May X experience well-being.' We repeat these aspirations several times, and each time we repeat them the identity of X changes. Traditionally, you begin by making all aspirations for yourself: 'May I be happy…' etc. Then you repeat the aspirations, making X someone you love. Then someone you are neutral about. And, finally, someone you dislike. In some variations, there's a further stage, where X is every sentient being in the world. A few teachers add yet another stage that encompasses the entire universe – sentient or otherwise.

On the surface this practice seems to be some kind of prediction of the future – or a demand, entitlement or request: make everyone happy! But it's vital not to get hung up on the supposed 'results' of the practice. The aspirations are not the important bit. The aspirations are simply there as a way of triggering something inside you. Their function is to make you focus on the feeling of love.

What matters in a loving-kindness meditation is not whether everyone you've wished happiness for actually becomes happier; what matters is what happens to you when you try to express love – especially for someone you dislike. Are you able to feel love, or are you not? This is the crux of the practice.

The practice is not designed to magically make everybody in the world constantly healthy, happy and free from suffering. It is designed to gradually soften and dismantle all the internal blockages that are stopping you from opening your heart.

As you try in this practice to send out positive loving feelings to someone you actively dislike, you will finally start to understand exactly what the phrase 'unconditional love' really means and, more importantly, just how difficult it is to make it happen (unless you are a truly extraordinary human being). It's quite likely that you will feel a gate coming down around your heart, a complete and utter resistance to any such thing happening.

The aspirations are very nice, but it is noticing that gate – understanding when it shuts and when it doesn't, and learning to keep it open for more of the time – that is the true work of the loving-kindness meditation.

WHO DO YOU LOVE?

There are stories that when the Metta practice was first brought over from the East to the West, students requested that the order be changed so that the practice began with somebody else – someone that the practitioner loved – rather than themselves. The teachers insisted that the reason the practice began with the self is that it's easier to love yourself than anyone else, but the students demurred, saying this simply wasn't true. They found it difficult to love themselves.

There was even a story of the Dalai Lama first encountering this Western concept of self-hatred and being completely baffled by it. Why would anybody not love themselves? Whether this story is true or not, it certainly *points* to a truth: in our modern society many people struggle with the idea of wishing themselves well or of offering themselves love. When I introduce a loving-kindness meditation in mindfulness classes, I routinely encounter people who find the first stage rather difficult or even completely impossible.

I've regularly encountered individuals who simply don't know where to start with this practice. When asked to locate the feeling of love within their body, they are unable to do so. *Where would that be? What would that feel like? How is this done?* The idea is so far outside their normal way of functioning that it seems impossible.

Even if this is you, even if you currently feel completely separated from love, there is no reason for things to stay this way. Just look at David Bowie, a man who had at one point in his life shut down his emotions, believing that love 'rotted' him, but who was later able to embark upon and maintain a long, loving marriage.

We'll look now at the Metta practice, and another practice for cultivating love. We'll focus especially on the starting point and make room for those who find it difficult to imagine taking part in a practice like this.

Even if all this talk of love isn't 'your kind of thing', consider trying these exercises anyway.

YOUR PATH

In this section you are going to do something that may sound quite daunting but is actually very simple. You are going to open your heart to love. This is not about finding love somewhere else in the world. It's about learning to *be* love.

We all have the ability to love. And we all have resistance and blockages that sometimes stop us from loving.

Our task is to find where we are blocked and give that place our kind, gentle attention so that we can slowly remove these blockages and open ourselves to love.

The exercises we're going to do are very simple and straightforward, but that's not to suggest they're easy. It's highly unlikely that you will be able to practice a loving-kindness meditation for the first time and instantly find yourself radiating love into the world. What is much more likely to happen is that you will encounter a series of points of resistance as you work through each stage of the exercises. This resistance is not a problem. It is what we are looking for. It indicates where the work needs to be done.

The loving-kindness meditation is not designed to be a peaceful moment of hippie loveliness. It's designed to be challenging work that will, over time, allow you to feel more love.

You may be thinking: hang on, surely love is not meant to be hard work? It's not the love that's the hard work. The challenge comes when we try to take apart the walls that we've constructed around our heart to protect ourselves in the past.

Before we embark on the full loving-kindness meditation, we'll work through another, simpler exercise called *Cultivating love.*

As we work through the exercises below, I have identified key ways in which you might meet resistance and suggested some strategies for working with that resistance. If you do not meet resistance of this particular kind, just ignore these strategies. Equally, if you meet resistance of a slightly different kind, you may find the strategies outlined will be useful to deal with your specific resistance.

Exercise: Cultivating love

Normally, when we feel our love for another person – someone special in our lives – it's just for a brief moment. Perhaps when we first meet them after a long absence, or when we hear their voice on the phone when we're apart, or when we're suddenly reminded of an important moment in our shared past.

Our heart fills with love.

We know this feeling. And we know that – for the most part – it doesn't last long. This feeling may last for fifteen seconds, maybe a bit longer. And then our thinking mind interrupts with the next thing we have to say or do or plan or worry about, and the feeling evaporates and it's back to 'normal'.

Yet we do not have to let this feeling disappear after fifteen seconds. We can hold on to it and allow it to grow. We can cultivate love. This exercise is designed to help you learn how to do this.

To begin this exercise, close your eyes. Think of somebody for whom you have unconditional love or who has unconditional love for you.

Now actively summon that feeling of love. You might do this by remembering a specific moment you spent together or simply by picturing their smiling face. Explore your memory to find the moment that triggers the feeling of love for them.

When you've conjured up the feeling, focus on it in the same way that you focus on your breath in a breathing meditation (*see page 23*): not *thinking* about it but simply being aware of it and maintaining it as the focus of your attention.

When you find you're distracted by thoughts and ideas (such as worrying about whether you are doing this exercise the 'right' way), do exactly as you do in the breathing meditation: label the thought as 'thinking', let it go and bring your attention back to the feeling of love.

You may find you are able to sustain the feeling of love for longer than you usually do. Perhaps on the first occasion you try this the feeling may last for thirty seconds; the next time you try, it may last for a minute, and so on. Repeat the exercise often, gradually building up your ability to cultivate and then sustain the feeling of love.

Possible resistance: I can't think of anyone who loves me or anyone that I love

Strategy 1 – If there is no one in the present who fits this category, think back over your past. If this still doesn't bring anyone to mind, understand that it doesn't have to be somebody who you absolutely, definitely, permanently, 100 per cent loved for ever and ever. For example, you might have a brother or sister with whom you have had a difficult, up-and-down relationship; however, you know that, when you were five and they were seven, they loved you. Go back to that moment, find a memory of a day that you were together when they were kind to you or took care of you. Use that as the trigger to summon the feeling of love.

Strategy 2 – Do you have or have you ever had a pet? A dog is a wonderful source of unconditional love and you can use a dog (or your memory of a dog) in this exercise as your trigger for love. Cats are not known for unconditional love, but if you're a cat person you may find you can use a cat in this exercise. Other pets can work too.

Strategy 3 – You can use a kind stranger to trigger the feeling. Simply think of someone who showed you a moment of kindness and focus on that moment.

Strategy 4 – Think of someone who you do not personally know but whom you consider to be a very loving or kind person. This could be a figure from the past, a great religious or spiritual leader or an inspirational person from today's headlines.

Possible resistance: I cannot locate the feeling of love

It's perfectly natural to hit an obstacle at this point. Up until this moment in your life, the feeling of love is something that seems to have simply happened to you. It has always been triggered by external events. You've never tried to just make it happen.

The idea that you can just make it happen might seem a bit 'fake' to you. *Am I really allowed to just summon up and luxuriate in such a wonderful feeling whenever I like? Do I deserve it?* Yes, you are. Yes, you do.

Or you might just not know what the instruction means. It's a bit like when you first attend a yoga or Pilates class and are told to relax a particular muscle. If you've never done that before, the instruction seems absurd. *How do I do that? How do I isolate one muscle? And how do I get it to relax?* But over time you learn.

The first thing to understand is that what I'm describing is perfectly possible. You *can* create this feeling yourself. Indeed, whenever you have felt love in the past, you have created the feeling yourself. There has been an external trigger, but *you* created the feeling. That's how feelings work. So you *do* know how to do it; you just don't know that you know how to do it.

Don't get stressed, don't worry and definitely don't struggle. We're not trying to force something to happen. We are trying to allow something to happen – something that can happen quite naturally.

Strategy 1 – At the start of the exercise, place a hand on your heart, on the centre of your chest. Take some time simply focusing on the contact between your hand and your chest. Note how this feels. Note how this changes: switch your attention between noting how your hand feels against your chest, and then noting how your chest feels against your hand. Practise switching between these two different perspectives. Initially when you try this exercise, simply hold your hand here and focus on this area without any expectations of any outcome. Simply focus on your heart in the way that we've previously focused on our breath. As thoughts arise, let them go. Simply stay with your heart. Over time, as you get used to this idea, gently try to access the feeling of love. Don't worry if nothing happens. You may have to do this *Connecting with your heart* exercise a few more times first.

Strategy 2 – Some people who are not used to this kind of emotional work find it helpful to ask themselves a slightly distancing question such as: 'What would it feel like for someone to feel love?' This is a gentle way of approaching the work – almost as an academic exercise: if someone was feeling love right now, what would that feel like?

Strategy 3 – Don't do this as a planned exercise, but instead simply wait till the feeling of love arises naturally in your normal life. Then, if appropriate, close your eyes, focus on the feeling, letting thoughts and other distractions go. Note where the feeling is in your body; note the texture of the feeling; note how it changes; as it lessens, note how this is experienced. Each time this happens, you will learn more about the feeling and be more able to summon it in the future.

Exercise: Loving-kindness meditation

We have our basic list of aspirations drawn from the Buddhist chants of the Four Limitless Ones: 'May X be happy and know the root of happiness. May X be free from suffering and the root of suffering. May X be safe and protected and free from harm. May X be healthy. May X experience well-being.' They include the slightly unusual construction 'the root of happiness' and 'the root of suffering'. The idea is that, as well as wishing that a person may be happy, we are wishing that they also understand the causes of happiness. It's a little bit clunky so we might take it out of our aspiration and take it as read that, in wishing happiness to someone, we are also wishing this additional level of understanding.

Sit quietly and relax. In some variations of this meditation, you're asked to close your eyes; others suggest you keep your eyes open. Just choose whichever you prefer.

Using whichever technique worked best for you in the previous exercises, awaken the feeling of love, then allow yourself to bathe in this feeling of love for a while.

Use our usual technique to maintain focus on this feeling: noticing when you're distracted, labelling the distraction, and then bringing your focus back to the feeling of love.

Become aware that, even though you might have used a memory of someone else to trigger the feeling, you are actually generating the feeling of love yourself.

Notice the purity of this unconditional love.

Say the aspirations to yourself one at a time, pausing to notice any change in the feeling or any resistance:

> May I be happy.
>
> May I be free from suffering.
>
> May I be safe.
>
> May I be healthy.
>
> May I experience well being.

If there is any slight resistance or any struggling, your task is simply to notice it, stay with it for a while, gently encouraging the resistance to soften, and then to continue the exercise. (If you hit stronger resistance, see the strategies below.)

Expand your field of awareness to include, as well as yourself, somebody you love. Say the aspirations for them. Stay with each line for a while, noticing how it affects the feeling within you.

Expand your field of awareness again to include somebody about whom you are neutral.

Say the aspirations for them. Notice how your feelings change.

Open your awareness even further to include someone who is problematic for you, someone who you actively dislike, perhaps someone who's harmed you in some way or someone you consider your enemy. You are not forgiving them or condoning their behaviour in making these aspirations. You are recognizing that they are human beings. They want to be happy and safe.

Everybody struggles and everybody suffers. Say the aspirations for them. Once again, notice how you react internally.

Now, open up your awareness to include everybody in the world.

Say the aspirations again for everyone. In doing this you are acknowledging our interconnectedness: that we're all united and that we have more in common than separates us.

If you want to you can add a further round of aspirations for the entire universe. You may feel that it doesn't make sense to say 'May the universe be happy'. If so, don't do this stage, or change the wording. On the other hand, you may find that you very much want to wish the universe some happiness.

The mindfulness pioneer Jon Kabat-Zinn expressed the thinking behind these last stages brilliantly when he said, 'what is most important is that we incline our own hearts towards inclusion rather than towards separation.'

Possible resistance: I don't like these phrases – they don't sound right to me

Strategy – Feel free to change the wording of the aspirations to something that makes sense to you. The important point is to keep the aspirations consistent as you expand your field of awareness.

Possible resistance: I thought it was going to feel great, but it just felt a bit mechanical

Because this meditation is based on a list of aspirations, it is quite easy to find yourself doing the exercise just like that – a list; you realize you are just ticking boxes without any genuine feeling. If this happens, spend more time on the initial stage, summoning the feeling of love. Be sure that you have this feeling 'in place' before you even begin the aspirations. Then slow the exercise right down, ensuring you are focusing on what is happening inside you at each stage, not on 'getting the words right'.

Possible resistance: I find it impossible to wish these nice things to myself

Strategy 1 – Change the order in which you do the exercise. Place yourself after the person that you find difficult.

Strategy 2 – Don't worry about the rest of the meditation. Simply stay with this resistance. This has now become your exercise. Just spend ten minutes staying with your resistance to loving yourself. After a while, explore whether you can wish yourself some compassion: 'May I be kind to myself in this moment.' If you find resistance to this too, ask yourself: 'If a friend of mine told me they were unable to wish themselves happiness or any kind thoughts, what might I say to comfort them?' Say this to yourself. If your friend deserves it, so do you.

Possible resistance: I don't want to wish loving kindness to my enemies

Remember, sending loving kindness is not a sign either that we forgive them for what they've done or that we condone their actions. Understanding this, try again or simply move on to the stage of wishing happiness to everyone. (Sneakily, of course, this includes all your enemies, but you may find it easier.)

Your path: Going forward

1. When feelings of love arise naturally in your life, try to remember to focus on them and sustain them using the techniques you have learned in this chapter. Why should it always be that the bad feelings last for hours, but the good ones are so fleeting?

2. Make loving-kindness meditation a regular part of your meditation practice. If you find a lot of resistance during the loving-kindness meditation, your task is simply to work with this resistance. Don't worry about 'finishing' the meditation or doing it 'right'. Just stay with the resistance for a few minutes. Occasionally, gently ask yourself: 'Can I soften a little now?' Even a very slight softening of resistance is a wonderful moment.

3. If difficult feelings arise in a loving-kindness meditation, remember you have the *REAL meditation* and *Tea with Mara* techniques (both from Chapter 7) in your emotional toolbox now to help you handle them.

Ask yourself: 'If I loved myself unconditionally what would be different?'

Ask yourself these questions:

How would someone who loves themselves unconditionally talk to themselves? Is this how I talk to myself?

What kind of relationships will somebody who loves themselves unconditionally have? Are my relationships like this?

How would somebody who loves themselves unconditionally treat other people? Is this how I treat other people?

How would someone who loves themselves unconditionally look after themselves? Is this how I look after myself?

You may think of your own variations. Don't be too hard on yourself about your answers, but do look for any positive changes you can make.

CHAPTER 10: WHERE ARE WE NOW?

The life lesson: Live your life as an enlightened being

Once I had all those big dreams. Oh, I had all those big dreams, man! I had them until I learned about simply enjoying the process of working, and the process of living.

(David Bowie)

Sometimes you will never know the true value of a moment until it becomes a memory.

(Iman – tweet on the day before Bowie died)

Give him back!

(YouTube comment following Bowie's death, under a video of Bowie performing 'Comfortably Numb' with David Gilmour at the Royal Albert Hall, 2006)

BOWIE'S PATH

Bowie's death was as inspirational as his life. To the end he was productive and creative, leaving the world with his wonderful *Blackstar* album. What can we learn from Bowie's final year?

Tony Visconti knew Bowie for forty-nine of his sixty-nine years. He worked with him before he was famous and was still at his side as a trusted collaborator on his final album, *Blackstar*, bonding over Buddhism as well as music, and sharing a teacher in Chime Rinpoche. From this uniquely informed perspective, Visconti says: 'In his final year, David was the happiest I had ever known him to be.'

That's something to aspire to, isn't it? To be at your happiest at the end of your life? And Bowie's final year was not an easy one – he was battling cancer. It says a lot for the man's spiritual and psychological growth that he could be happy at the end of his life under such circumstances. But then one of the (many) ways in which Bowie departed from our cultural norms was in his continual willingness to engage with the fact that we are all mortal. Bowie had always gazed directly at death.

We've met the great Tibetan Buddhist master Milarepa regularly in this book. One of the stories about this legendary figure from the Kagyu lineage that fascinated Bowie and Visconti was his commitment to charnel ground practice. In Tibet, in areas where the ground is so hard that burying bodies is impractical and fuel for cremation scarce and expensive, the dead are given 'sky burials'. Behind this elegant euphemism is the stark fact that the bodies are simply left on the surface of the earth. These are the charnel grounds.

Milarepa famously practised meditating at night in these charnel grounds, surrounded by bodies starting to decompose, skeletons picked clean by the scavenging local animals and everything in between.

Such contemplation is designed to help the participant – or perhaps that should be *force* them – to confront their fear of death. Sitting in the cold, looking at bodies, smelling bodies, hearing the calls of the animals, they face in the most vivid and visceral way imaginable the reality that one day they will be like this.

YOU ARE GOING TO DIE. NOW, HOW WILL YOU LIVE?

Why such grim practices? In Buddhist belief – and other traditions – it is thought that you will not be truly happy, and will not truly understand how to live, until you have genuinely contemplated your death, totally accepting that your body will one day be a corpse. You have to completely understand that – in Frank Close's terminology – the atoms that currently think they are you will one day change their minds and decide that in fact they are something else.

Crucially, when Buddhists say that everything is impermanent, this includes you.

To a modern Western sensibility, the idea of charnel ground practice may seem quite shocking. It challenges our concept of spiritual work (it turns out it's not all candles, incense and cushions, beatific smiles and elegantly flowing robes), and it is the exact opposite of the way our culture approaches the fact of death. We hide death away; we go out of our way not to think about it. Many of us, for much of our time, pretend it's just not going to happen to us. Collectively we set up society in such a way that we rarely have to think about it, leaving it very much to the professionals. Individually we set up our lives so that we are too busy to think about it, too surrounded with distractions to ever have a moment to remember that one day all of this stops.

Bowie, on the other hand, stared death in the face from a young age. At the age of twenty he was writing songs like 'Please Mr Grave Digger' and 'Conversation Piece', which concern respectively murder and suicide. Murder remained a theme in his songs from 1970's 'Running Gun Blues' through to 2013's 'Valentine's Day'. His 1995 album *1. Outside* is themed round a murder, while the subject matter of 1974's *Diamond Dogs* is genocide.

In live shows, at the peak of his early fame as Ziggy Stardust, when he was a young, dynamic twenty-five-year-old playing to audiences of teenagers, he would interrupt the glam-rock hits to sing a slow, haunting version of Jacques Brel's 'My Death', a song which takes the listener through three long verses packed with imagery of darkness and decay, ephemerality and extinction. In an interview in the *Big Issue* in 1997 he told his interviewer, Jarvis Cocker, 'I can't think of a time that I didn't think about death.'

In the video for 'Lazarus', before Bowie backs into the wardrobe, he sits at a desk writing feverishly in a notebook. At his side is a skull.

Bowie the book-lover and autodidact will have been well acquainted with Saint Jerome, the patron saint of scholars, librarians, students, archivists, and encyclopaedists. Bowie the art-lover will have been well aware that Saint Jerome was traditionally depicted in paintings writing at his desk accompanied by a skull. Indeed, many of the hand gestures and body shapes that Bowie adopts in this brief scene seem to mirror paintings of the saint.

In the paintings the skull is there as a symbol to remind Saint Jerome of his own mortality and of the fact that he had limited time to get his work done. It is also there, of course, as a prompt to the viewer. Sadly, Bowie didn't need symbols; it was while he was filming the 'Lazarus' video that he was told by his doctors they would be stopping treatment for his cancer. He knew he was dying.

The skull, then, is there for us. The message is simple: you are going to die. Now, knowing this, how will you live?

The skull and the allusion to Saint Jerome sit among a riot of symbolism and imagery. It would take a whole book to run through all the possible interpretations of the lyrics of Bowie's songs 'Blackstar' and 'Lazarus' and the imagery that Bowie and his director Johan Renck put into the accompanying videos. But what is most immediately clear is that the lyrics and images highlight a concentration of references to the esoteric practices Bowie was investigating in Los Angeles in 1975 – the extraordinary mixture of alchemy, Gnosticism, Kabbalah and magic we explored in Chapter 6. It seems that, at the end of his life, Bowie had returned to a fascination with the Gnostic idea of what he termed 'the God beyond God' – the Kabbalist's Ein Sof.

Of course, we must not get too carried away with our symbol hunting. The idea of a black star has alchemical significance, but there is also a brand of guitar amps called Blackstar. It's entirely possible that Bowie – with his love of 'found' lyrics – simply saw the name in the studio one day and thought, 'That would make a good title.'

However, the one image that is entirely unambiguous is the dead astronaut. If you see an astronaut in a Bowie video (and you do – frequently – in 'Ashes to Ashes', 'New Killer Star' and 'Slow Burn' as well as 'Space Oddity' and 'Blackstar') then that will be Major Tom.

WHATEVER HAPPENED TO MAJOR TOM?

'Space Oddity' is arguably Bowie's most misunderstood song. The assumption is that it's a sad song in which an astronaut is literally lost in space, unable to return to Earth. In 1980's 'Ashes to Ashes', Bowie – having lived through his own mid-1970s drug hell – reinvented the character as a junkie, but this was not the original hidden meaning of the song. While on one level written to commercially capitalize on the recent moon landing, 'Space Oddity' is at its heart, according to its author, a metaphor for the Buddhist concept of enlightenment, which Bowie was learning about from Chime Rinpoche.

If you get hold of a copy of the original *Space Oddity* album (the one with a permed Bowie on the cover, not the post-Ziggy, red-haired reissue) and turn to the back cover you will see a drawing of Chime – underlining how important his teacher was to Bowie's life and music at this point.

That Buddhist enlightenment is a central meaning of Major Tom's experience is made clear in an interview Bowie gave to Mary Finnigan that appeared in the counterculture *International Times* shortly after the release of the song. Finnigan reprinted much of the interview in her book *Psychedelic Suburbia*, which documents the period in the 1960s when Bowie was a tenant in her house, working on pre-fame projects like the Beckenham Arts Lab. Discussing 'Space Oddity', Bowie makes it clear that Major Tom isn't lost at the end; he is free. Bowie explains that Tom has gone beyond our world of conceptual thought and arrived at a place where 'he is everything'. Major Tom is not a tragic figure; he is an enlightened individual.

Forty-four years later, when Bowie broke a ten-year silence with the unexpected release of 'Where Are We Now?', he was returning to the same subject. Like 'Space Oddity', there is an obvious story on the surface of the song – in this case, a travelogue through Bowie's Berlin memories – but again there is another level. While the verses concern themselves with Potsdamer Platz, the Dschungel nightclub where Bowie and Iggy hung out and KaDeWe where they bought their groceries, the chorus contains a simple message about the nature of enlightenment, tied to the song's title, which echoes the questions that Chime asked his students and that we have pondered throughout this book.

Who are you?

Where are you?

Where are you going?

Bowie, it seems, had found a place of much greater contentment and equanimity than he had enjoyed earlier in his life; his journey of self-discovery had been successful. But where are *we* now? And where are we going? If we pursue the quest of self-discovery outlined in this book, where could we finally get to? Where is our end point?

THE LIFE LESSON: LIVE YOUR LIFE AS AN ENLIGHTENED BEING

Where does our journey end? The end point of the Buddhist journey is enlightenment. Can we hope to reach such a state? Even if this seems too extraordinary a goal, we can certainly commit to living in a more enlightened way.

In the *Bowie's Path* sections of this book we have been following what Bowie termed his 'life's search'. You have echoed this quest with your own journey of self-discovery using the exercises in the *Your Path* sections. But if you are on a journey to discover your true self, how will you know when you find it? When can you say you've arrived?

There are arguably two answers, reflecting the two levels of reality we discussed in Chapter 8. You will remember that, according to Buddhist thought, these are:

> *Relative reality*: the reality that we perceive around us and that we normally live in – the reality that (until you start reading books like this) you consider the *only* reality
>
> *Absolute reality*: the true nature of things, which we can only appreciate when we stop our chattering mind and rest in pure awareness. In this reality the idea that we are

separate dissolves and we feel connected to all people and all things

In relative reality our task is to strengthen our conventional sense of self, while in absolute reality our task is to hold that sense of self much more loosely. These sound like contradictory aims but in fact they are entirely compatible. The two ideas work surprisingly well together. You actually need a strong sense of self before you can truly appreciate the 'no self' world of absolute reality.

So how do we know when we have reached the end of our journey?

WHERE ARE WE GOING? (PART 1): RELATIVE REALITY

In the world of relative reality we can chart our progress fairly easily. To discover if you've reached the place you need to be, simply review the work you've done so far in the following areas:

- the work on befriending your inner critic from Chapter 5
- the work on meaning and purpose in Chapter 6
- what you have learned about your shadow side in Chapter 7
- the work on values in Chapter 8
- the insight into your emotional life gained in Chapter 9.

If you have worked through the exercises in all these areas, then you have reached your destination. It's not a final end point but it's certainly a very good temporary stopping point. The reason it's not an end point is that you can usefully review this work on a regular basis. We will look at how to do this in the *Your Path* section below under the heading *Annual review*. And by the way, you don't have to wait a year to carry out this review; you can review your progress whenever you wish. In fact, you may find it helpful to run through the *Annual review* questions right now, before we shift our focus to the frankly trickier, vaguer and harder-to-measure world of absolute reality.

WHERE ARE WE GOING? (PART 2): ABSOLUTE REALITY

We have already discovered that the wisdom traditions that fascinated Bowie express our life's quest in different ways. It is variously termed the search for our true self or our true nature, a journey towards individuation or enlightenment, or (in Nietzsche's phrase) the will to become the Übermensch. In alchemy, it is known as the Great Work.

Different schools of thought agree that the Great Work involves seeing beyond our usual sense of separation and discovering a greater feeling of connectedness, but the thing we are supposed to feel more connected to is given many different names. We may be told that we are looking for our connection with nature, or with the universe, or with the divine, or just with 'everything'. We are variously encouraged to resonate with the energy that created the world, to look within for the kingdom of God, or to reunite the microcosm with the macrocosm.

If you dig deeper you will soon discover that, within each tradition, each individual teacher will also add their own unique terminology: you may find yourself listening to people talk about radiance, light or energy; you may find you are being encouraged to open up, to let go, to rise up or to drop down, to embrace the numinous or the luminous, to transcend and go beyond while also staying firmly in the now.

The language and terminology can sometimes be baffling, but what stays consistent is the idea that we need to awaken out of a world of illusion to grasp the true nature of ourselves and the world around us. So let's try and wade through the confusing language to more clearly define what this awakening might consist of. However many traditions you study, however many teachers you listen to and however many variations of awakening you hear about, I believe they can all be found within the following categories.

Intellectual awakening

This, in essence, is the understanding that you are not your thoughts. We explored this idea in Chapter 5, noting that many wisdom traditions state that as long as we are lost in our conceptual thoughts we cannot possibly understand reality. We are only ever seeing a filtered, biased and incomplete version of the world, and similarly we only ever see an incomplete version of ourselves. This type of awakening involves reaching a place where we can see the world and ourselves without any conceptual thoughts. No labels. No language. Pure awareness of what is.

In doing this we could say we are going back to the way we functioned in very early childhood, or that we are going back to the way human beings functioned before they developed language. As soon as we have language we have conceptual thought, and as soon as we have conceptual thought we start categorizing everything around us as separate objects, and separating ourselves from the rest of the world. We therefore have a fundamental barrier between ourselves and awakening.

Can we function in our day-to-day world without thought or language? No, of course not. But we need to be able to switch out of this way of functioning to see true reality. And when we *are* functioning in the world of thought and language, we need to retain a deep understanding that what's going on in our thoughts and with our language is always the map and not the territory.

Emotional awakening

This awakening involves the discovery that you can open your heart in those moments in life when you would normally close it, that you have the deep ability to always be open to love and not to close down against it.

When we explored this in Chapter 9, we realized that, although it sounds wonderful, it can in fact be extremely hard work. The modern world trains us every day to close down more, to construct a layer of armour around our heart to protect ourselves. The process of opening up once more to love may take many years – a reminder that, for most of us, awakening to reality is usually a long and gradual process with plenty of tangents, detours and setbacks.

Conceptual awakening

This involves the understanding that we are not separate beings, but rather are interconnected with the entire universe. The necessary shift in perspective could hardly be more extreme – we *seem* so separate. The best explanation of how we can be so clearly distinguishable as separate beings and yet still connected to everything else is probably that provided by Alan Watts:

> You are a function of what the whole universe is doing in the same way that a wave is a function of what the whole ocean is doing.

Each wave is distinct from those around it and yet obviously also a part of the ocean. As Watts pointed out, you can't put a wave in a bucket and carry it off. In a similar way we can be both visibly distinct and yet also connected to everything around us. In Buddhism, this is part of the concept of no self. In Gnosticism, this is the understanding that we are all simply expressions of the God beyond God – Ein Sof – as is everyone and every other thing in the universe.

SHOULD WE SEEK ENLIGHTENMENT?

Some people experience these awakenings as 'flashes' or 'glimpses' but then quickly return to normal ways of perceiving the world and their normal behaviours. Others seem able to hold on to this new way of seeing the world for longer. If someone experienced all three awakenings and was able to stay permanently in all three states – outside of thought, with their heart fully open, and with a genuine felt experience of their interconnectedness – they would surely have attained that most elusive of Buddhist states: enlightenment. They would be a fully realized being.

Other definitions of an enlightened being include someone who has rid themselves of all attachment – and therefore of all suffering. But we must be clear that this does not mean that nothing else ever goes wrong in their life. They may get ill, they may have to deal with many setbacks, they will surely suffer loss, but they have the equanimity to greet life's inevitable low points with an attitude of acceptance, so they do not suffer. Yet another definition of someone who has attained enlightenment is someone who no longer has any fear of death – the ultimate acceptance.

Enlightenment is the end point of the Buddhist journey. The Tao of Bowie – the path of discovery outlined in this book – began with Bowie's study of Buddhism, so if the Tao of Bowie has a destination, surely this is it? But is it? Is enlightenment actually a goal that we can actively work towards?

Traditionally, we're used to hearing about monks who practise for decades in a bid to attain enlightenment, meditating for eight or twelve hours a day, seven days a week, year after year. But are they right to do so?

There is a famous story of a Western man who approached a Zen master and asked, 'If I study with you how long will it take me to become enlightened?'

'Ten years,' replied the Zen master.

'No, you don't understand,' said the man. 'I'm not your average guy. I've got an MBA. I made my first million by the time I was twenty-five. I get things done. How long will it take *me* to reach enlightenment?'

'Oh,' said the Zen master. 'You're right. I *didn't* understand. For you, enlightenment will take twenty years.'

'No, no, no,' said the man. 'You're not getting it. I'll work 24/7. I'll hire assistants to do the grunt work for me. I'll pay you however much you want. I'll give you the money to build a new temple. All you have to do is turbo-charge the whole process. Now... how long?'

'Ah,' said the Zen master. 'Now I truly see. Forty years.'

So we have the idea that to reach the end point of our spiritual journey will take a huge amount of work. Yet we also have the idea that the more we work, the more we strive, the further away it will recede. Is the person who makes a huge effort to attain enlightenment pushing enlightenment further out of their reach simply by making all that effort?

To try to answer that, let's step back two further generations in Bowie's Buddhist lineage to meet Chime and Chögyam Trungpa's teacher, Khenpo Gangshar Wangpo, and *his* teacher Jamgon Kongtrul of Shechen.

... OR ARE WE ALREADY WHERE WE NEED TO BE?

There is a text written by Khenpo Gangshar, *A Song to Introduce the Unmistaken View of the Great Perfection*, in which he gives instructions for a simple meditation to help notice thoughts and rest in the space between them. It's very similar to (although far more elegantly phrased than) the exercise that appears in Chapter 1 of this book. This simple meditation was our starting point, but Khenpo Gangshar seems to suggest it could also be our end point. At the conclusion of the text, he states very clearly: 'there is nothing greater than this understanding'.

Certainly, we could conclude that if you get no 'further' in your journey of self-discovery than being able to step outside your thoughts – to understand what they are and, more importantly, what they are not – you will have achieved a lot. You will have a much clearer answer to the question 'Who are you?' because you will know you are not that endless chattering in your head. This alone is a transformative awakening.

When Chögyam Trungpa was nine years old, he received direct teachings from Jamgon Kongtrul. The lessons he received from this master were simple and informal – in marked contrast to the rigid practices of some of his other teachers. In their first lesson Jamgon Kongtrul told his young student that they would simply sit and do nothing. For the second lesson he suggested they sit and do nothing again, but also notice that they were breathing and follow the breath. Emboldened by the relaxed nature of the sessions, the nine-year-old Chögyam Trungpa asked the venerated master, 'What about enlightenment?'

'Oh,' said Jamgon Kongtrul matter-of-factly. 'There is no such thing as enlightenment. This is it.'

Both of Bowie's teachers' teachers seem to be saying, then, that there is no greater goal, no more precious attainment than the very simplest of meditation practices. That if we can simply sit, follow the breath, let thoughts go, and be truly in the moment, then we have already arrived at where we need to be.

Both are echoing a comment attributed to the Buddha by the ninth-century Zen master Huang Po: that when the Buddha attained complete enlightenment, he 'attained nothing'.

For anyone pursuing – or thinking of pursuing – the Buddhist path to self-discovery, this is one of the most confusing barriers. Are we engaged in a long and difficult path to enlightenment, or are we not?

Should our voyage of self-discovery be, as Bowie once suggested it was, 'a stubborn, painful trek' or are we, as Jamgon Kongtrul appeared to say, already where we need to be? Could someone just clarify this, please?

Possibly not. Possibly we simply have to live with the uncertainty. In the Christian mystic tradition, this is sometimes termed 'the cloud of unknowing'. It is the idea that, in order to come into full union with God, you must let go of any idea of what God is. We find something similar in Hinduism, where Brahman – the source of all existence – is described using the form *neti, neti*: not this, not that. Perhaps Khenpo Gangshar and Jamgon Kongtrul are saying something along the same lines: in order to attain enlightenment, we must give up any idea of what enlightenment is.

… OR DO WE NEED TO GO AWAY AND COME BACK AGAIN?

Another explanation of how Buddha could have attained enlightenment and yet attained nothing lies in the concept of 'Buddha nature'. It is said that we all already have Buddha nature (the *capacity* to be enlightened). All we actually need to do is realize that we have it and we're there. All we need to do is agree with Jamgon Kongtrul that 'this is it' and it will be.

Cool… except Buddha didn't just get out of bed one morning and think, 'I've attained enlightenment, but I've attained nothing.' It took him six years of relentless ascetic practices and then seven weeks of continual meditation and a mighty battle with the demon Mara in order to attain this enlightenment. That sounds an awful lot like a stubborn painful trek.

Perhaps rather annoyingly, given his statement that he attained nothing, it also sounds like a stubborn painful trek that ends up back where you started with the realization that you already had what you were looking for (so maybe the trek wasn't really necessary).

But then, perhaps without the trek you can't be sure that 'back where you started' is where you need to end up. Although wise people might tell us that this moment is all we need, maybe we need to check out everything else for ourselves before we can be sure that we agree with them.

... OR SHOULD WE JUST WALK ROUND AND ROUND IN CIRCLES?

Carl Jung suggested another variation. Recalling his personal development between 1918 and 1920, he said: 'I began to understand the goal of psychic development is the self. There is no linear evolution. There is only a circumambulation of the self.'

So where *are* we going? According to Jung, what we're doing is essentially walking round and round the self – continually gaining new perspectives and therefore new insights into who we really are. And, crucially, into who we are not.

As we go round and round in circles, we gradually let go of mistaken ideas about ourselves.

We let go of thoughts.

We let go of our emotional armour.

We let go of the need to be at the centre of the universe.

We let go of the struggle.

Because, as Chögyam Trungpa said: 'There is no need to struggle to be free; the absence of struggle is in itself freedom.'

'SIMPLY ENJOYING... THE PROCESS OF LIVING'

Bowie did have at least one happy childhood memory. He loved the song 'Inchworm' performed by Danny Kaye. There is a lot to love about the song. The composer, Frank Loesser, created a sublime melody with an intricate and delightful counterpoint. Bowie freely admitted that he used the song as an inspiration in many of his own works (most obviously as the basis for the unconventional rhythm that underpins 'Ashes to Ashes').

And then there is the lyric: on one level it is a simple childlike nursery rhyme; on another level, however, the song contains a central message that Bowie would go on to encounter in his Buddhist studies: that instead of busying itself with its measuring duties, the inchworm should pause and consider the beauty of the marigolds.

As Bowie intimated in the quote that opens this chapter, one of the most important things we need to learn is 'simply enjoying… the process of living'. This is how an enlightened person behaves – always fully alive to the wonder of the moment, the mystery of the world, the beauty of the marigolds. But we don't have to 'attain enlightenment' – *whatever* that means – to be able to do this. We can simply choose in each moment to behave as an enlightened being would.

In the next section, we will look at some simple guidelines to help you do that.

YOUR PATH

Here is a chance to review the work you have done throughout the book, and also some simple guidance for how to behave as an enlightened being.

This section has two parts. The first part is a suggested annual review of the work that you have done using the exercises in this book, which relates most closely to the world of relative reality. In the second part we will venture into the world of absolute reality and explore what it might mean to live your life as if you were an enlightened being.

PART 1: ANNUAL REVIEW

Instead of bothering with those (inevitably soon-to-be-broken) New Year's resolutions, why not use the lull between Christmas and New Year's Day – this natural annual period of reflection – to look back over your year, and ask yourself the following questions?

Values, purpose and meaning

When have I really lived up to my values?

When have I veered away from my values?

When have I most felt a sense of purpose?

When have I most felt that my life had meaning?

Bearing in mind your answers to the above questions, determine what tweaks you could make in your life to ensure you spend more time aligned to your values, living with purpose and finding meaning in what you do. If you're not clear how to do this, refer back to the *Your Path* sections of Chapters 6 and 8.

Are there any areas where a tweak would clearly not be enough? If you think you need to make major changes, ask yourself if you need the support of others to achieve this, and identify people who can help you.

Heart and mind

Have I been able to develop my ability to feel love? If not, where were the triggers that stopped me? How could I do more work in these areas?

Have I been able to respond skilfully or have I got lost in thought? If I've been getting lost in thought, what are the situations where this happens most often? How could I do more work in these areas?

If you need further clarity on any of these questions, refer back to the *Your Path* sections of Chapters 5 or 9.

This process is about accountability not blame. Do not beat yourself up for every time you have failed to live up to your values or got lost in thought. Everybody fails to live up to their values from time to time. Getting lost in thought is so easily done. Instead give yourself credit for the times when you have lived up to your values (and give yourself credit for going through this annual review).

Make some commitments going forward, but make them commitments to do more work in certain areas, rather than commitments to hit specific targets. Do not set up a narrative of success or failure.

PART 2: LIVING AS AN ENLIGHTENED BEING

No more exercises – just some simple guidelines.

As we've seen, definitions of enlightenment vary widely. Some say we are all enlightened (although we may not realize it), while some believe enlightenment is a very rare and special condition that only a tiny percentage of people can reach. However, whether we are enlightened or not – whether we are even clear on what our definition of enlightenment is – we can make simple choices in each moment to behave in a more enlightened way. We do not need to attain a specific state in order to behave as an enlightened person might behave at any one moment.

Can we truly have the presumption to say that we know how an enlightened person would behave? Well, no, we can't be 100 per cent sure. But there are certainly enough clues in the wisdom traditions we've explored in this book to give us a pretty good idea of when we are behaving in a more enlightened way and when we are doing the opposite.

Digging into these traditions, we've unearthed some powerful ideas that can guide your behaviour on a daily basis. Among them:

- Don't take your thoughts so seriously.
- Hold your sense of self very lightly indeed.
- When you meet your edge don't tighten – soften.
- Stay open to love.

Each one of these ideas has the potential to nudge you towards a more enlightened way of living.

Now let us turn to one last guide to help us with our future behaviour. If we trace the Tibetan Kagyu lineage back to its origins in India, we encounter Tilopa.

Tilopa gave a very succinct teaching called the Six Words of Advice. In their most usual English translation, the instructions grow to being slightly more than six words, but they remain simple, clear and powerful:

- Let go of what has passed.
- Let go of what may come.
- Don't think.
- Don't try to figure anything out.
- Don't try to make anything happen.
- Relax right now, and rest.

Tilopa urges us not to live our lives in the future; nor should we live in the past. He advises us to let go of thought and stay in the present moment in simple awareness. He suggests that we let go of our desire to control and instead learn the value of acceptance. Finally, he tells us to stop struggling and simply relax.

As you read the Six Words of Advice you might have wondered if this is advice for how to meditate or advice for how to live. The answer is: both. Certainly, these words would help you approach your meditation with the right intention. But also, in any moment, these words of advice will guide you towards more enlightened behaviour.

Although when you first start meditating it seems to be a totally separate activity from the rest of your life, over time this distinction should become less clear. One thing we can be sure that an enlightened person would do is carry the attitudes and qualities of their meditation with them into what Buddhists call 'post-meditation' and what the rest of us call 'life'. And so, if there is one idea above all others that I would urge you to take from this book, it is the importance of a regular meditation practice.

Every day, take a few moments.

Pause.

Follow your breath.

Let your thoughts go.

And then – as Bowie's teacher's teacher, Khenpo Gangshar, put it – 'rest in the utter brilliance that is the space beyond thought'.

ACKNOWLEDGMENTS

The Buddhist theory that we are not separate selves but are fundamentally interconnected with all other beings is usually difficult to grasp, but when you try to write the acknowledgments for a book, it suddenly becomes glaringly obvious. If I truly traced all the individuals on the long and winding journey that led to the creation of this book, there would quickly be thousands of names. So I'll limit this to those who were directly involved in making this book happen.

While this is not primarily a work of original research, a series of interviews with early students of Chime Rinpoche and with Bowie's long-term collaborators have been extremely helpful in either revealing or confirming the teachings that Bowie most likely received and outlining how he applied them to his life. Particular thanks to Ron Ede, Derek Henderson, Carlos Alomar and Tony Visconti.

As someone who has spent decades getting briefly excited about one supposedly 'great idea for a book' after another without actually *writing* any of them, I owe a huge debt to the two Clares for making this time different: to Clare Grist Taylor, my agent, for helping me conceptualise, package, sell and write this book (it's a delight to be a client of The Accidental Agency); and to Clare Drysdale, my editor at Allen & Unwin, for carefully guiding someone who usually stops after a thousand words through the daunting process of writing closer to 70,000.

I'm also indebted to everyone else at Allen & Unwin who has worked on the book. This includes – but I'm sure is not limited to – Alice Latham, Aimee Oliver-Powell, Kate Straker and Richard Evans.

Also thanks to Charlotte Atyeo for catching my mistakes in the copy-editing process.

And to Noma Bar for designing the cover (oh, the cover!) and Ben Cracknell for typesetting.

Finally, thanks to Sue, Sylvia and Georgia for their encouragement when listening to half-formed ideas and their advice when acting as first readers of some early drafts.

FURTHER READING

A comprehensive reading list for some of the subjects covered in this book, such as Buddhism or the Kabbalah, could prove to be as long as the book itself. So here are just a few suggestions as starting points for further reading, should you wish to pursue any of the ideas discussed in the preceding pages.

David Bowie

Reference and Biography

The Complete David Bowie, Nicholas Pegg, 2000

Rebel Rebel, Chris O'Leary, 2014

Bowie: Loving the Alien, Christopher Sanford, 1996

Alias David Bowie, Peter Gillman and Leni Gillman, 1987

Starman: David Bowie the Definitive Biography, Paul Trynka, 2011

David Bowie: A Life, Dylan Jones, 2018

Themes and Periods

Heroes: David Bowie and Berlin, Tobias Rüther, 2008

Bowie in Berlin: A New Career in a New Town, Thomas Jerome Seabrook, 2008

Psychedelic Suburbia: David Bowie and the Beckenham Arts Lab, Mary Finnigan, 2016

When Ziggy Played Guitar: David Bowie and Four Minutes that Shook the World, Dylan Jones, 2018

David Bowie: Fame Sound and Vision, Nick Stephenson, 2006

David Bowie: Critical Perspectives, edited by Eoin Devereux, Aileen Dillane and Martin J Power, 2015

Upping your Ziggy, Oliver James, 2016

More general books that contain insightful essays/sections on Bowie

In Other Words, Anthony DeCurtis 2005.

Bowie, Bolan and the Brooklyn Boy: The Autobiography, Tony Visconti, 2007

All the Madmen, Clinton Heylin, 2012

Buddhism

Early Buddhist texts and the masters of the Kagyu lineage

The Life and Teaching of Naropa, Herbert V Guenther, 1995

Tilopa's Mahamudra Upadesha: The Gangama Instructions with Commentary, by Sangye Nyenpa, 2014

The Mind of Mahamudra: Advice from the Kagyu Masters, Peter Alan Roberts, 2015

The Heart Attack Sutra: A New Commentary on the Heart Sutra, Karl Brunnhölzl, 2016

Gampopa, Ornament of Precious Liberation, translated by Ken Holmes, 2017

The Hundred Thousand Songs of Milarepa, Tsangnyon Heruka, translated by Christopher Stagg, 2017

More recent figures

Meditation in Action, Chögyam Trungpa, 1970

Vivid Awareness: The Mind Instructions of Khenpo Gangshar, Khenchen Thrangu, 2011

When Things Fall Apart: Heart Advice for Difficult Times, Pema Chödrön, 2005

Zen

The Way of Zen, Alan Watts, 1957

Zen Mind Beginner's Mind, Shunryu Suzuki, 1970

Zen Keys: Guide to Zen Practice, Thich Nhat Hanh, 1998

The Zen Teachings of Huang Po on the Transmission of Mind, translated by John Blofeld, 2006

Carl Jung

Modern Man in Search of a Soul, Carl Jung, 1933

Memories, Dreams, Reflections, Carl Jung, 1963

Meeting the Shadow: Hidden Power of the Dark Side of Human Nature, edited by Connie Zweig and Jeremiah Abrams, 1990

Jung's Map of the Soul, Murray Stein, 1999

Jung and the Alchemical Imagination, Jeffrey Raff, 2000

The Red Book: A Reader's Edition, Carl Jung, 2009

Consciousness and the development of thought

Thought and Language, Lev Vygotsky, 1934

The Discovery of the Mind: In Greek Philosophy and Literature, Bruno Snell, 1948

The Origin of Consciousness in the Breakdown of the Bicameral Mind, Julian Jaynes, 1976

The User Illusion: Cutting Consciousness Down to Size, Tor Norretranders, 1991

The Minds of the Bible: Speculations on the Cultural Evolution of Human Consciousness, James Cohn, 2013

Gnosticism

The Gnostic Gospels, Elaine Pagels, 1979

Gnosis and Hermeticism from Antiquity to Modern Times, edited by Roelof Van Den Broek, 1998

The Nag Hammadi Scriptures, edited by Marvin Meyer, 2009

The Gnostics: Myth, Ritual, and Diversity in Early Christianity, David Brakke, 2011

Magic

The Key of the Mysteries, Eliphas Levi, 1861

Psychic Self-Defense, Dion Fortune, 1930

The Hermetica: The Lost Wisdom of the Pharaohs, Timothy Freke and Peter Gandy, 2008

Perdurabo: The Life of Aleister Crowley, Richard Kaczynski, 2010

Kabbalah

The Mystical Qabalah, Dion Fortune, 1935
Meditation and Kabbalah, Aryeh Kaplan, 1982
Kabbalah: New Perspectives, Moshe Idel, 1990
On The Kabbalah & Its Symbolism, Gershom Scholem, 1996
Thirty-Two Gates: Into the Heart of Kabbalah and Chassidus, Rav Dovber Pinson, 2019

Alchemy

Alchemy Ancient and Modern, H Stanley Redgrove, 1922
Alchemy: Science of the Cosmos, Science of the Soul, Titus Burckhardt, 1967
Alchemy: The Medieval Alchemists and their Royal Art, Johannes Fabricius, 1976
Hidden Wisdom: A Guide to the Western Inner Traditions, Richard Smoley and Jay Kinney, 1999
Alchemy & Mysticism, Alexander Roob, 2014

Nietzsche

The Gay Science, Friedrich Nietzsche, 1882
Beyond Good and Evil, Friedrich Nietzsche, 1886
Nietzsche's 'Zaraathustra': Notes of the Seminar given in 1934-39, Carl Jung, edited by James L Jarrett, 1988
Composing the Soul: Reaches of Nietzsche's Psychology, Graham Parkes, 1996
What Nietzsche Really Said, Kathleen Higgins, 2000
Hiking with Nietzsche, John Kaag, 2018